LEAVEN

LEAVEN

150
WOMEN IN
SCRIPTURE
WHOSE LIVES
LIFT OURS

JERRIE HURD

ASPEN BOOKS

Leaven: 150 Women in Scripture Whose Lives Lift Ours
© 1995 by Jerrie Hurd
All rights reserved
Printed in the United States of America

Library of Congress Cataloging-in Publication Data
Hurd, Jerrie W.
Leaven: 150 women in scripture whose lives lift ours / Jerrie Hurd
p. cm.
Includes index.
ISBN 1-56236-220-8
1. Women in the Mormon sacred books. I. Title.

BX8627.3.H87   1995   95-6361
289.3'2'0922--dc20   CIP

Cover design: Richard Erickson
Cover illustration: *Jesus and Woman of Samaria* by Gustave Doré

To my mother,
Colleen Nielsen Wirkus Purcell

TABLE OF CONTENTS

Why I Care about My Sisters in the Scriptures

I wanted to know what a prophetess was.

I was fifteen years old, and I knew there were prophetesses in the Old Testament, and I wanted to know what those women had done to make the writers of sacred script single them out as "prophetesses." Back then I asked the question over and over again with great insistence of my Seminary teacher, my Sunday School teacher, my Young Women's teacher, my mother's friends, my friends. No one seemed to know what to say. I got shrugs, funny looks, mumbled explanations about women being good wives and mothers, and one whispered aside from an elderly woman in my ward who told me I'd understand when I went to the temple because ladies were called "priestesses and queens" in the temple, and then she added, "but they might not always be treated that way."

Those answers did not satisfy.

I did not understand then that my question had deeper roots. I wanted to know what a prophetess was because I couldn't articulate what I really needed: exciting, uplifting examples. I literally churned inside because it seemed to me that a prophetess must be something special—something worth celebrating with a wonderful title. I wanted to know how to live my life with that kind of extraordinary verve.

I'm not sure how I satisfied my fifteen-year-old yearnings. I don't remember. Time moved on and other things became more important . . . until my father died.

He was only fifty-two years old and his death was somewhat sudden. I was a young mother at the time. Standing at his graveside following his funeral, I realized I still wanted to know what a prophetess was. Only this time, I knew the question was a mask for my need to know my own potential.

I was already a mother, and I felt I was a good mother, but I was thirty-one years old. What else could I expect to achieve? How did I go about shaping my life beyond the role of being a mother, which was clearly demanding but not all encompassing? Even though I understood the question better, I still didn't have an answer.

I began asking again. Friends. Home teachers. Visiting teachers. An old BYU professor. My bishop, who told me there was no doctrine about prophetesses, only a couple of stories. My insistence was not fueled by insolence. I was truly searching for a way to create myself, discover myself. I wanted to get my roots down to "living water."

2

It was slow in coming, but I finally realized that no one was going to answer that question for me. So I began to study the scriptures. And I began with the stories of my sisters in the scriptures because that's what I needed to nurture my own growth.

I had read the scriptures before. I had disciplined myself as we are told to do. For long periods in my life I had read a chapter a day faithfully. This was different. This time I approached the scriptures as a quest, and the words took on life. Page after page came to me with startling clarity, creating new light in my understanding, warmth in my soul.

My first and perhaps most amazing discovery was that I never fully appreciated the uniqueness of the Mormon view of Eve. I hadn't separated what the restored gospel teaches from the larger Judeo-Christian tradition. It is an important difference. For while other Christians and Jews pine for the perfect world lost when Eve sinned, members of the restored Church rejoice along with our first mother. In Moses 5:11, Eve exclaims, "Were it not for our transgression we never should have had seed, and never should have known good and evil, and the joy of our redemption, and the eternal life which God giveth unto all the obedient." In other words, knowing what the consequences would be, Eve dared do what was needed that her children might be born.

The purpose of creation was to provide physical bodies for God's spirit children and give them experiences that would allow them to distinguish good from evil. Eve's eating the forbidden fruit furthered that purpose. As such, it was a necessary and brave act.

It's probably a peculiar personal quirk, but I've been refashioning fairy tales since childhood. Take the story of Cinderella. I could never figure out why the tale of that poor chambermaid was so focused on the prince. He never did anything. It was the fairy godmother who changed the pumpkin into a carriage! And I wanted to know how she did it.

Understanding the true role of Eve, as explained by the restored gospel, is just as startling. It makes all the difference. Suddenly I felt a new thankfulness for the coming forth of the Book of Mormon, Doctrine and Covenants, and Pearl of Great Price.

In Genesis, Eve is declared "good" along with the rest of God's creations. But more than that, in the Book of Abraham she, along with Adam, is given charge over all the earth (Abr. 4:27–31). The idea that the man is not without the woman nor the woman without the man is outlined in the Genesis account of creation, but we cannot begin to comprehend the full meaning of the eternal marriage of a man and a woman in their quest for exaltation until we turn to scriptures of the restored gospel (see D&C 132:19–20). Such scriptures do not imply that a man shall rule over a woman but that they will counsel together as partners, for one cannot be greater than the other—they must become "one" together. In fact that is the celestial order. Clearly Adam did not rule over Eve before they fell. Now, as we seek to live higher, celestial lives, we must seek to emulate the pre-Fall condition, not perpetuate the fallen one.

3

Yes, Eve transgressed first, and yes, Eve's transgression caused the Fall that left us alone in this dreary world. But she did not partake of the fruit because she was weaker or more easily tempted than Adam. Restored doctrine rejects the notion that women are largely at the mercy of the desires of their flesh—temptresses to be avoided unless one be tempted also.

No, Eve was an agent fully capable of making the single decision that would most affect mortality. Satan knew that. He didn't dangle the fruit in front of her like some pretty bauble. He offered, instead, some rather sophisticated arguments for why she might choose to disobey Father.

In the Garden, the man and the woman were not ashamed or even aware of their nakedness. But once they had eaten, they "saw" their differences. They had fallen into a new order, a world of opposites, a world of good and evil. Called to answer for the sin, Adam blamed Eve: "The woman whom thou gavest to be with me, she gave me of the tree, and I did eat." And Eve blamed the snake: "The serpent beguiled me . . ." (Gen. 3:12–13). Somehow their transgression had disrupted the most fundamental relationship in the world—that between man and woman.

Nevertheless, despite their attempts to assign blame, the Lord required both to be accountable. In the Doctrine and Covenants we are told that "the devil tempted Adam [implying the couple, Adam and Eve], and he partook of the forbidden fruit" (D&C 29:40). In the Book of Mormon, Nephi tells us that "Adam fell that men might be" (2 Ne. 2:25), and King Benjamin explained the natural man's love of evil in terms of "the fall of Adam" (Mosiah 3:19). Eve could easily be included in such verses, for in restored scripture the *couple* is responsible. They acted in concert, not individually. Knowing that, one can see that even in Genesis the man is never separated from the woman.

So as a Latter-day Saint familiar with my own scriptures, I know that Eve did not frustrate the plan of God. Rather, I owe her respect for her courage, which ultimately allowed me, her daughter, to be born. And I know that she was forgiven for her transgression in the Garden of Eden (see Moses 6:53). What's more, the restored gospel forbids belief in "original sin." We do not baptize babies, nor do we believe, as the Jews of old, that women are unclean vessels that must be cleansed after giving birth. Our second Article of Faith clearly states that "men will be punished for their own sins, and not for Adam's transgression." That also applies to women and Eve's transgression. To believe that women are weaker, inferior, or must be punished for what Eve did would negate Christ's universal atonement. I bring no sin with me into this world, and I alone am responsible for working out my salvation.

That is a far loftier view of our mother Eve and women in general than the world at large holds. It is a freeing and ennobling vision. But I had to know my own scriptures before I could unshackle myself from the traditional opinion.

What's even better, the Doctrine and Covenants tells me that along with her faithful daughters, my "glorious Mother Eve" is hard at work organizing, instructing, and preparing the spirits of the next world (see D&C 138:39).

Let me give you another example of how my view of a woman found in scripture changed as I continued to study.

I had thought Rebekah was a deceitful woman. After all she tricked her husband into blessing her favorite son, Jacob, instead of his favorite, Esau. Still I liked her. I thought she was clever and showed a certain independence of mind.

Careful reading only reinforced my opinion of Rebekah's spirited independence. When Abraham's servant Eliezer appeared at her village well looking for a wife for his master's son, Rebekah answered, "I will go." When her family wished for her to remain with them for a few more days, while Eliezer wanted to leave immediately, Rebekah sided with Eliezer. She seemed to know her own mind, or was it more than that?

Eliezer felt that finding Rebekah was a direct answer to prayer. Were her strong feelings similarly motivated?

The dimensions of Rebekah's spirituality do not become clear until she is pregnant and her pregnancy is not going well. Then the scriptures show her seeking the Lord in prayer, asking, "Why am I thus?" Speaking directly to Rebekah, the Lord answered, saying: "Two nations are in thy womb, and two manner of people shall be separated from thy bowels; and the one people shall be stronger than the other people; and the elder shall serve the younger" (Gen. 25:23).

Suddenly my picture of Rebekah shifted. The ability to hear the word of the Lord in our minds and hearts is the Spirit of Prophecy, and obviously here was a woman spiritually attuned enough to receive that kind of direct answer to her prayers. What's more, I realized from this recorded incident that Rebekah knew before her children were born that the younger, Jacob, was to receive the greater blessing. Knowing that, how could a mother have stood by and let her husband give the blessing to the wrong child?

Isaac had lands, wells, flocks, and servants that represented great worldly wealth that he could give away only once. He also had the blessing of his father Abraham, the spiritual covenant, which he couldn't give away at all, unless it was to a worthy recipient. Isaac had a worthy son and an unworthy son, but he loved them both. So in his desire to keep the law of the firstborn, Isaac may have thought he could bless Esau first and bestow upon him the worldly wealth, the double portion due an oldest son, and then later give Jacob the covenant blessing. But Rebekah challenged that.

Perhaps she knew that Esau with his limited spiritual perception would not understand the difference and claim forever the right to the covenant and thereby confuse the covenant lineage. At heart, Isaac and Rebekah were not seriously divided. The blessing Isaac conferred upon Jacob, when he thought he was Esau, was not the blessing of Abraham. There is no mention of Abraham in it, or of the land that had been promised to Abraham's seed, or of a multitude of descendants. When the deception was exposed and Esau asked for a blessing, Isaac promised that his "dwelling shall be the fatness of the earth, and of the dew of heaven from above" (Gen. 27:39), giving him essentially what he had intended all along; it was only Esau who felt cheated. But his anger was real enough. He vowed to kill his brother as soon as their father was dead.

Rebekah, always decisive, knew something had to be done. Now that the "birthright" son had been designated, she could have had Esau expelled. Instead, she gave up her beloved Jacob, sending him off to her father's house in Padan-aram to find a wife there. As he was leaving, Isaac blessed Jacob a second time, declaring, "And God Almighty bless thee, and make thee fruitful, and multiply thee, that thou mayest be a multitude of people; And give thee the blessing of Abraham, to thee, and to thy seed with thee; that thou mayest inherit the land wherein thou art a stranger, which God gave Abraham" (Gen. 28:3–4). That was the blessing of Abraham. Isaac gave it to Jacob knowingly.

In saying good-bye to Jacob, Rebekah was hopeful: "Flee thou to Laban my brother . . . and tarry with him a few days" (Gen. 27:43–44). But she would never see her favorite son again. His tarrying with her brother Laban "a few days" would stretch out twenty years, and she would die before he returned.

Before my careful reading of her story, I hadn't realized the sacrifice Rebekah made in sending her son away. But more importantly, through my own efforts at scripture study, I had discovered a determinedly spiritual woman who still had the power to lift lives—my own.

The importance of knowing my sisters in the scriptures came to me one day as I sat in a Sunday School class listening as the teacher attempted to explain the prophetess Huldah. Uncomfortable with the concept of a "prophetess," because he didn't understand it, he was saying that King Josiah sought Huldah's opinion on a religious matter only because Israel had fallen into such waywardness there was no one else to consult but this woman. Years before when studying Old Testament in gospel doctrine classes, I had heard other teachers, men and women, struggle with Huldah. More than once I had felt troubled by their stumbling over her story, ignoring it, or sometimes suggesting, as this teacher was that it was beneath a king to ever have to seek a woman's advice. Yet in times past, I had said nothing. I hadn't known what to say. I hadn't done my scripture study. But this time I knew he was wrong, and I asked if I could tell Huldah's story.

Far from being the only person King Josiah could have consulted, Huldah lived at a time when many prophets were crying repentance in Jerusalem. According to the Book of Mormon, Lehi may well have been one; from other scriptures we know that Jeremiah was another; so was Uriah. But King Josiah had a particular problem that required a particular kind of expertise—someone who could evaluate ancient documents.

While renovating the temple, King Josiah's workers had uncovered a manuscript containing religious law. The high priest had read parts of it to the king, leaving him uneasy about the message those writings contained. So he ordered his high priest and his chief scribe to respectfully go and call upon Huldah and ask her to authenticate it. Remember, he was a king. He could have ordered her to

8

appear before him, but instead he sent his servants to her to consult with her as a prophetess.

Huldah is described as being the wife of Shallum, whose family kept the king's wardrobe, but a distinction is made between her and her in-laws, saying that she "dwelt in Jerusalem in the college" (2 Kgs. 22:14). Presented with the scrolls, Huldah declared the writings to be scripture—scripture the people had forgotten and then lost. In fact, part of that manuscript is now found in Deuteronomy. Then, as a prophetess Huldah went on to prophesy, in the name of God, that Jerusalem would be destroyed because the people had forgotten and disobeyed the laws contained in that manuscript. But because the king had humbled himself and sought to know the true word of God, she promised him that he would be gathered to his fathers before her prophecy came to pass.

King Josiah was impressed. He had been a righteous king before, but now impelled by Huldah's words, he assumed the religious leadership of his entire nation. First he had the newly found book of law read publicly. Then he extracted a new commitment from his people to live those laws. After that, he destroyed the shrines of the heathen gods and re-instated the Levites. The people improved, but shortly after King Josiah's death they again lapsed into unrighteousness, and the remainder of Huldah's prophecy was eventually fulfilled.

But the respect people felt for Huldah continued. Six hundred years later, at the time of Christ, two gates to the temple were still being called the Huldah Gate One and the Huldah Gate Two in honor of this woman.

Following that Gospel Doctrine class, I had many individuals, including the teacher, thank me for sharing the contribution of Huldah. Maybe that's one reason why President Spencer W. Kimball urged women to become "sister scriptorians,"[1] and President Howard W. Hunter said,

Some women long for that inspiration which can comfort the heart, bind the wounds, and give knowledge sufficient to point the way when there seems no reliable way to turn. But we are not left comfortless! We have the scriptures, which contain enduring words of a loving Father in Heaven, who tells us that we are his first priority.[2]

In this dispensation, Joseph Smith stated that he felt the restoration of the gospel was not complete until he had organized the women. At one of the first meetings of the Relief Society he said, "and I now turn the key to you in the name of God and this Society shall rejoice and knowledge and intelligence shall flow down from this time."[3] Eliza R. Snow, who became our second General Relief Society President and happened to be at the meeting when Joseph Smith made that statement, felt that the prophet had put Latter-day Saint women "at the head of all the women of the world."[4]

Later, in 1945, President George Albert Smith told women that "when the Prophet Joseph Smith turned the key for the emancipation of womankind, it was turned for all the world, and from generation to generation the number of women who can enjoy the blessings of religious liberty and civil liberty has been increasing."[5] For me this is consistent with Doctrine & Covenants 61:17 where at the beginning of this dispensation, God, who had once cursed the earth, now blesses it so that his Saints (both men and women) can freely partake of all that creation has to offer.

Searching the sacred texts for the women portrayed there is only one way to explore the richness the scriptures have to offer. Any honest search will be rewarded. In his Sermon on the Mount, Jesus urged his followers to seek after truth, promising that those who seek will find. He went on to add, "What man is there of you, whom if his son [daughter in my case] ask bread, will he give him a stone?"

He then notes, "If ye then, being evil, know how to give good gifts unto your children, how much more shall your Father which is in heaven give good things to them that ask him?" (Matt. 7:9, 11).

My earthly father sometimes struggled to understand me, his daughter. But he knew how to give a good gift. He gave me life. He gave me a liberal portion of his German stubbornness. He taught me how to work. He let me believe it was okay to question and never quit until you had an answer. While he didn't exactly show me the way, he gave me what I needed to find my own way. That is bread. My Heavenly Father's gifts are manna.

This brings me to Shelly, a young woman who plopped herself down in class one day and proceeded to file her nails as I began that Sunday's lesson. I was a substitute teacher, and she was visiting from another ward. I don't believe in coincidence. She was seeking, and the Lord had given her—me.

Halfway through a lesson that had failed to spark much interest in any of the young women, Shelly straightened herself and said: "Why don't we ever talk about prophetesses or interesting stuff like that?"

The question was out of context, thrown as a gauntlet—a challenge. I had done it myself at her age to watch the teacher squirm or look stupid.

I closed the lesson manual. "Which one of the prophetesses would you like to talk about?"

She stammered. "I—I don't know—the prophetesses. You know."

"Yes, I do," I said. "Shall we start with what it means to be a prophetess?"

Suddenly I had the attention of everyone.

I went on to explain that the term *prophetess* is confusing because it is used several different ways in the Old Testament. Sometimes it is an honorary title given to the

11

wife of a prophet. That was true of Isaiah's wife and Ezekiel's wife. The word can also mean a woman who writes poetry, just as the Hebrew word *prophet* can mean a man who writes poetry. The Old Testament is full of great poetic works, and anciently the ability to express oneself in poetry was considered a spiritual gift.

The word *prophetess* also refers to a few women who possessed the power to prophesy, who declared that they spoke God's message, and whose prophecies were fulfilled. These women include Miriam, Deborah, Huldah, Anna, the four young women mentioned in the book of Acts (21:9), and probably others not named.

I explained that priesthood ordination is not a prerequisite for possessing this gift. It is one of the gifts of the spirit that worthy members of the Church have been repeatedly urged to seek (see 1 Cor. 12:10; 14:39; Omni 1:25; Moro. 10:13; D&C 46:22). Prophecies can be spoken by men and women, adults and children. Moses outlined in detail how a woman could take on the vows of a Nazarite (see Num. 6:2-8), and when Jesus visited the Nephites, he opened the mouths of babies who then spoke things too wondrous to be recorded (see 3 Ne. 26:14).

Most important, I explained that the Old Testament prophet Joel saw a time when "your sons and your daughters shall prophesy" (Joel 2:28). The angel Moroni repeated that scripture to Joseph Smith at least three times, saying that it was about to be fulfilled.

I told Shelly and those other young women that I hoped they would be part of fulfilling Joel's words.

When she left, Shelly hugged me.

That's why I care about my sisters in the scriptures. They are enduring examples with the power to lift lives—mine, Shelly's, others. Their stories, full of variety and verve, suggest possibility and potential.

God provides amply for his children, including many,

many ways to be spiritually enlightened. I have experienced the power of prayer, fasting, blessings, the words of ancient and modern prophets, counsel from spiritual leaders and family. From the scriptures I have been enriched by sermons, prophecies, poetry, instructions, and the accounts of men as well as women.

Beyond that, I, personally, needed examples that put a womanly face to mortality's challenges. And as usual, God provided. The women in scripture offer not only their example, but their strength. I had only to look.

Notes

[1] Spencer W. Kimball, *Ensign*, May 1978, pp.5–7
[2] Howard W. Hunter, *Ensign*, November 1994, p. 96.
[3] See Relief Society Minutes of Nauvoo 28 April 1842.
[4] See Smithfield Ward, Cache Stake Relief Society Minutes, 12 May 1878.
[5] See address in *Relief Society Magazine* 32, Dec. 1945.

13

How to Read the Scriptures and Not Miss the Women

A Quick Course

STEP # 1
LOOK FOR THE REFERENCES TO WOMEN

This is an obvious first step, yet important. Too often words like *sister, wife, mother,* etc., are missed. But if we take note, such references to women will complete the scriptural cast, giving us a rounder, fuller picture. We discover that Nephi had sisters as well as brothers (2 Ne. 5:6), that the role Pharaoh's daughter played in preserving the baby Moses was foretold (JST Gen. 50:29), and that Noah's granddaughters were partly responsible for the evil that preceded the flood (see Gen. 6:1-4; Moses 8:14-15).

Small vignettes also emerge from the texts—little stories that add richly to the understanding of how God works to aid his children. For example, the story of Pharaoh's midwives is contained in a mere eight verses at the beginning of the book of Exodus and yet suggests larger significance.

According to this story, Pharaoh first tried to limit the population of Hebrew slaves by calling in his chief midwives, two women named Shiphrah and Puah, and giving them new orders. He said, "When ye do the office of a midwife to the Hebrew women, and see them upon the stools; if it be a son, then ye shall kill him: but if it be a daughter, then she shall live" (Ex. 1:16).

He seemed to think that too many young men might be

armed and turned against the Egyptians, but young women could continue to work and serve their masters without creating that kind of fear. How did Shiphrah and Puah respond to Pharaoh's suggestion? They agreed to do as they were instructed. If they had refused, they would have been removed from their offices and others more willing to carry out those instructions would have been found.

But then the scriptures say that Shiphrah and Puah "feared" God more than Pharaoh and didn't do as they had been told (Ex. 1:17). However, in those days no one defied Pharaoh and lived. Inevitably someone was going to notice all the little Hebrew boy babies running around and call it to Pharaoh's attention.

Sure enough, Shiphrah and Puah were summoned by Pharaoh again and asked, "Why have ye done this thing, and have saved the men children alive?" (Ex. 1:18). What could they answer? They looked Pharaoh in the eye and told him the Hebrew women were "more lively" than the Egyptian women and had their babies before the midwives could get there. And Pharaoh believed them! Not only did he keep the midwives in their offices, but the scriptures say that God prospered these women and made them "houses"—meaning many descendants.

15

This is a story with human drama and an element of humor. But there are larger dimensions.

Scholars have noted that this incident is the first recorded use of nonviolent resistance. When Moses freed the Hebrews and led them out of Egypt, he did not arm the young men and fight his way out, as the Pharaoh had feared. Rather, with the help of God, he brought plague after plague upon the Pharaoh and his land until he was forced to let them go. Where did Moses learn about nonviolent resistance? Was it the same place Shiphrah and Puah learned it? Is this why their story is found just ahead of Moses' story?

STEP #2
ASK WHY A PARTICULAR
REFERENCE HAS BEEN INCLUDED

Considering how many times the Bible has been edited and condensed, I have to assume that the surviving references to women must have been considered important. In the case of Shiphrah and Puah, the story is clearly more than a clever example of courage. It is a powerful story of faith, of fearing God more than man, and of a number of other things. That is true of other examples. In fact, asking why a reference has been included can produce some startling revelations. Consider the story of Jehosheba.

Jehosheba is mentioned briefly in Second Kings (11:2) and again in Second Chronicles (22:11 as Jehoshabeath). The wicked Queen Athaliah, following her mother Queen Jezebel's example, had been actively encouraging the worship of idols and supporting the priests of Baal while persecuting believers of the one true God. When her husband and sons died, Athaliah realized her influence at court was about to end. Rather than allow that to happen, she ordered that all her grandsons be put to death, leaving her next in line to rule. Her order was carried out with one exception—Jehosheba, wife of the high priest Jehoiada who officiated over the temple, grabbed one of Athaliah's grandsons, fled the royal nursery, and hid with him in a bed chamber until she was able to take him to the temple where he was hidden for years until he could be declared the rightful king.

Again this is a story that can be admired for the courage exemplified. Jehosheba risked her own life to save the baby who would become the next king and who would rule in righteousness and undo much of the wickedness of his grandmother. But there is an even deeper significance. If Queen Athaliah had successfully destroyed all her grandsons, she would have put an end to the royal house of David, effectively preventing the fulfillment of many prophecies concerning the birth of the Messiah.

One of only three women named in the Book of Mormon is a Lamanite serving woman called Abish (Alma 19). What makes her important? Her story is told so briefly she is often overlooked in favor of Ammon and his missionary brothers. Yet, on closer examination, it seems likely that Ammon and his brothers may have had nothing to tell were it not for Abish.

The scriptures describe Abish as a Lamanite woman who had been "converted unto the Lord for many years, on account of a remarkable vision of her father" (Alma 19:16). She is also described as being a servant in the household of the Lamanite King Lamoni. Not much else is known about her. Yet the success of the mission of the Sons of Mosiah to the Lamanites comes to pivot on the quiet, patient faith of Abish—who may have influenced King Lamoni's household, servants and royal family alike.

I'm sure your remember how Ammon and the other three sons of Mosiah renounced their father's throne to go preach the gospel to the Lamanites. After fourteen years of labor, they converted thousands who gratefully took upon themselves the name of Ammon, calling themselves "the people of Ammon." But initially, Ammon and his brothers were not successful or even well received. In fact, they were all thrown into prison.

Ammon had separated from his brothers and found himself serving King Lamoni, tending his sheep. One day he was able to miraculously save the king's sheep from robbers and that created the opportunity Ammon had been waiting for. When the king, awed at Ammon's superhuman power, asked how Ammon was able to perform miracles, Ammon began to explain the gospel, beginning with the creation of the world. The king was so overcome by what Ammon was teaching that he fell into a spiritual swoon and appeared to be dead. When the king was still unconscious after two days, some advisors suggested to the queen that he ought to be buried, but she summoned Ammon instead.

She explained that her servants (possibly Abish and those she may have enlightened with her example) had told her that he was a prophet who could do mighty works in God's name. Then she asked about her husband. Was he dead?

Ammon assured her that the next day—the third day—her husband would rise again. Then he asked, "Believest thou this?" Her answer was simple and direct, "I have had no witness save thy word and the word of our servants; nevertheless I believe" (Alma 19:9).

Twice more this queen will express a willingness to believe Ammon because she has the word of her servants. Clearly something about her servants impressed the queen to the point that she was willing to accept their explanations of what was happening. Could it have been that Abish had prepared King Lamoni's household in some way to receive the true gospel? When the king awoke, he preached the gospel to his wife and family and the other servants. They were baptized—the beginning of the Church among the Lamanites.

Once King Lamoni had been converted, he was instrumental in the conversion of his father, the king over all the Lamanites, and in getting Ammon's brothers freed from prison so they could begin their missionary work. Their success among the Lamanites caused them to be known as the "great missionaries of the Book of Mormon," and yet their successes, nearly every success they had, can be traced directly to the royal household of King Lamoni and the serving woman Abish. Without her, the story might have been very different.

STEP #3
PULL THE PARTS OF STORIES TOGETHER

Sarah, Abraham's wife, is a good example of why pulling

the different parts of a story together is a necessary step. The scriptures present several verses about Sarah, then several chapters about Abraham, followed by several more verses about Sarah. As a reader, I tend to forget what I knew about Sarah while I'm reading about Abraham. As a result, I may finish reading without forming a clear impression of Sarah or her contributions. But if I mark and read the various references to Sarah all at once, I discover that she emerges as a distinct personality, a full partner to the great Abrahamic promise.

The story of Lot's offering his daughters to appease the men of Sodom cannot be understood without reading both the original Genesis account and the Joseph Smith Translation of the same events (see Gen. 14:16; 19, and JST Gen. 19:9–5). In the Genesis account, Lot, who is described as a righteous man, seemingly offers his virgin daughters to a lecherous mob of Sodomites in order to spare his guests—a troublesome notion not satisfactorily explained by the laws of hospitality which required that the head of a household defend any guest who had sought protection under his roof. Joseph Smith corrects and elaborates on the story, indicating that the mob requested both the daughters and the guests, intending to rape the women and sodomize the men. Lot refused both requests.

Women whose stories are better understood if the parts are pulled together include Sariah from the Book of Mormon, Rebekah, Miriam, Mary the mother of Jesus, and others. One woman, Eve, is mentioned in all four standard works, including a quote from her testimony (see Moses 5:11–12). In fact a complete understanding of our first mother requires knowing the scriptures restored by Joseph Smith. The fact that he greatly increased the number of verses referring to this woman suggests the importance of fully appreciating her role.

19

> ### Joseph Smith Greatly Increased
> ### the Verses Referring to Eve
>
> | EVE IN THE BIBLE | EVE IN THE RESTORED SCRIPTURE |
> |---|---|
> | Genesis 1, 2, 3, 4, 5 | 1 Nephi 5:11 |
> | 2 Corinthians 11:3 | 2 Nephi 2:18–25 |
> | 1 Timothy 2:13 | Mosiah 16:3 |
> | | Alma 12:21, 26; 42:2–7 |
> | | Helaman 6:26 |
> | | Ether 8:25 |
> | | Moses 2, 3, 4, 5, 6 |
> | | Abraham 4, 5 |
> | | D&C 20:18–20 |

STEP #4
UNDERSTAND SACRED TITLES

Do you know what it means to be . . .

> *a Prophetess?*
> *a Wise Woman?*
> *a Handmaiden of the Lord?*
> *a Mother in Israel?*
> *an Elect Lady?*

Besides being known as mothers, wives, daughters, and queens, women are often given sacred titles in scripture. While it is not always possible with each individual reference to determine exactly what a particular title means, clearly these were terms of honor and can be understood as patterns emerge that suggest meanings.

The most confusing is the title *prophetess*.

It seems to have been used with a variety of meanings. As I explained earlier, it is sometimes the honorary title given to the wife of a prophet; it sometimes means a woman who writes poetry; but most often it is used to honor women who possessed the gift of prophecy. These include Deborah, Huldah, Miriam, Anna, the four daughters of Philip, and in modern times Eliza R. Snow, who was named a prophetess by Joseph Smith. False prophetesses are also named in scripture (Neh. 6:14; Ezek. 13:17–18), just as there are false prophets.

The scriptures tell of two *wise women*: The Wise Woman of Abel (2 Sam. 20:16–22) and the Wise Woman of Tekoah (2 Sam. 14:1–20). The title seems to be applied to women who advised kings and generals. Sometimes it seems synonymous with *prophetess*.

More women are called a "handmaiden of the Lord." Ruth, Hannah, Abigail, and the Wise Women of Tekoah were all referred to by this term. In one of his psalms (see Ps. 86:16), King David refers to himself as the "son of a handmaiden," honoring both himself and his mother with the title. In the Doctrine and Covenants, Emma Smith and Vienna Jaques (see D&C 132:51-55 and 90:28) are each designated a handmaiden of the Lord. Although the use of this term is never clearly defined, most of these women willingly made great sacrifices—Hannah returned her child to serve in the temple; Mary willingly took on the responsibility of bringing the Savior into the world; Vienna Jaques donated all her worldly wealth to the Church; etc.

21

The title *Mother in Israel* was an honor many women desired. That is why many barren women in ancient scripture are described as "mourning before the Lord." They yearned to be mothers. Moreover, anciently the term also seems to have been recognized legally. Tamar defended her actions before a council of elders by pointing out that her right to her children had been denied her by her father-in-law (Gen. 38). The Wise Woman of Abel turned back an army by shaming them for coming against a Mother in Israel (2 Sam. 20:16-22).

Handmaidens

RUTH *(Ruth 2:13)*

HANNAH *(1 Sam. 1:11)*

KING DAVID AS SON OF HANDMAIDEN *(Ps. 86:16)*

ABIGAIL *(1 Sam. 25:24)*

WISE WOMAN OF TEKOAH *(2 Sam. 14)*

MARY, THE MOTHER OF THE SAVIOR *(Luke 1:38)*

HANDMAIDS WHEN SAVIOR COMES AGAIN *(Joel 2:29; Acts 2:18; Joseph Smith History 1:41)*

EMMA SMITH *(D&C 132:51–56)*

VIENNA JAQUES *(D&C 90:28)*

Joseph Smith explained the title *elect lady*. Although his wife, Emma, had been named an elect lady years earlier in the revelation now known as Doctrine & Covenants 25, it was on the day she was made president of the newly formed Relief Society that her husband defined the term: to be an elect lady was to be elected to a particular calling in the Church. In New Testament times, the Apostle John wrote a letter to another elect lady rejoicing that her children had been true and faithful (see 2 John). She may have been John's wife. He also refers to the first woman's "elect sister." Both women seem to have been faithful and involved in the affairs of the early Christian church, as John was.

That same Apostle John saw the Virgin Mary in a vision that would become part of his book of Revelation (see Rev. 12:1). Of all the sacred titles and all the great honors given women, Mary's is the greatest. The Angel Gabriel greeted Mary saying: "Hail, thou that art highly favoured, the Lord is with thee: blessed art thou among women" (Luke 1:28).

STEP #5
BE AWARE THAT SOME PASSAGES
MAY NOT SEEM FLATTERING TO WOMEN

I am referring to more than the examples of unrighteous women, of which there are plenty. Women like Queen Jezebel, the daughter of Jared, and the Witch of En-dor actually balance the picture, showing that women's choices do matter and that women are capable of evil as well as good. The reader can learn from their examples as well as the examples of righteousness.

Passages that are more troublesome are those that state unequivocally that a woman is worth less than a man, or imply that her female nature is evil or more prone to embrace evil, or that she can be bought and sold as chattel. For example, the Lord spoke to Moses and defined the values of various individuals, crops, flocks, etc. in order that the person or property might be redeemed with the proper tithe. The value placed on a woman was 30 shekels while a man was valued at 50 shekels (see Lev. 27). Another part of the Law of Moses states that a woman's natural bodily functions—menstruation and childbirth—are unclean (Lev. 12). Likewise, under certain circumstances women were required to prove virginity; men were not (see Deut. 22:13–21).

In the New Testament, the Apostle Paul also wrote a number of verses that seem bothersome. In First Corinthians, he suggests women keep silent in church and cover their heads when they pray, though the translation of these particular passages is in question. But you don't have to be a student of ancient languages to get a broader perspective. Instead of focusing on these difficult verses, note how many women Paul greets throughout his letters, praising and commending them. Also note that while Paul expresses a preference for women wearing a covering on their heads when they pray and prophesy, the idea that they will be praying and prophesying is taken for granted—even expected.

In all cases these troublesome passages need to be understood within the context of the culture of the time and also within the larger context of God's dealings with men and women over thousands of years. God has always blessed both men and women, urged his prophets to address both their concerns, answered their prayers, opened visions and sent angels to administer to both alike. Repeatedly the Lord has urged men to love their wives and women to love their husbands. Children are urged to honor their fathers and their mothers, and prophets have warned that nations will be judged by how well widows are cared for.

Restored scripture also helps put a proper perspective on these passages. In his letter to the Galatians, Paul writes that all are equal in Christ—male and female, bond and free. But in the Book of Mormon, Nephi states even more emphatically,

> and he doeth nothing save it be plain unto the children of men; and he inviteth them all to come unto him and partake of his goodness; and he denieth none that come unto him, black and white, bond and free, male and female.
> (2 Ne. 26:33)

Similarly, Alma describes the Church in his day as "having no respect to persons" (Alma 1:30).

Even more interesting are the number of prophetic scriptures that use feminine imagery. Many of the prophets of the Old Testament personified Zion as a woman—the woman of the Lord's choosing. At the Second Coming, this Zion becomes the "Lamb's bride," an idea echoed in Jesus' telling of the parable of the ten virgins.

Noting the verses that offer positive, glorious imagery and comments about women and their role in the eternal scheme can also help to balance and place the troublesome passages in perspective. But there are other passages that are not so much troublesome as they are just plain hard to understand.

STEP #6
TAKE TIME TO FIGURE OUT
DIFFICULT PASSAGES

> *Arise and thresh, O daughter of Zion: for I will make your horn iron, and I will make thy hoofs brass: and thou shalt beat in pieces many people: and I will consecrate their gain unto the Lord, and their substance unto the Lord of the whole earth. (Micah 4:13)*

If you are looking for references to women, you can hardly miss the fact that Micah 4:13 seems to be addressed to the daughter of Zion. But who is the "daughter of Zion?" What is this passage about? The verse doesn't offer much meaning from a casual reading. To understand more fully, you must study it out.

Almost any public library will offer a variety of Bible commentaries. Most agree that Micah 4:13 is about the nations that try to destroy purified Israel in the last days but that are destroyed by Israel instead. That means this is not a passage about women.

The term daughter of Zion is a poetic symbol for Jerusalem. In Hebrew, cities are considered feminine, and so feminine symbols are used repeatedly throughout scripture to represent Jerusalem—more often the New Jerusalem, the purified, holy spiritual center of the Millennium. That seems to be the case for this passage and similar passages in Isaiah, Jeremiah, Moroni, etc.

However, poetic devices often encompass more than one level of meaning. In many passages the daughter of Zion is described as sitting down in dust or putting on garments, things a city cannot do but which its citizens, its women, can do, suggesting that a more literal interpretation may also be possible.

Furthermore, Micah 4:13 is interesting because of its context. Scholars familiar with the doctrine and additional scriptures of the restored Church have traditionally read the entire chapter of Micah 4 quite differently from other Bible scholars. The accepted understanding of Micah's prophesy centers entirely on Jerusalem and the building of the temple there in the last days. However, when most Mormons read "But in the last days it shall come to pass, that the mountain of the house of the Lord shall be established in the top of the mountains; and it shall be exalted above the hills; and people shall flow unto it" (Micah 4:1), they envision the Salt Lake Temple and the missionary work of this dispensation that is gathering Israel in preparation for the Second Coming. Quite a different notion.

It is possible for both interpretations to be true. It is the layers of possible meaning that make scripture study both challenging and exciting.

What's more, if one were to extend that modern-day interpretation of Micah's prophesy to include verse 13, one might see in that passage a description of the role of women in the latter-day missionary work. To arrive at this meaning, we must define the unfamiliar phrases. For this you will need to consult a Bible dictionary—a larger and more complete volume than the Bible Dictionary bound into the LDS scriptures. The phrases "Arise and thresh," "make thine horn iron," "make thy hoofs brass," and "consecrate their gain" can be understood fairly quickly from such a dictionary, available at almost any public library.

The result is possibly a wonderful promise to the women of the latter days. Paraphrased, the verse seems to say: Arise and do missionary work, O daughter of Zion, and I will give you success (iron horn) and endurance (brass hooves) and you will harvest many peoples and bring them to the Lord.

If that interpretation is one possible understanding of Micah 4:13, it has a certain resonance with an address President Spencer W. Kimball gave in 1978. In that speech, he states several times that people will be drawn to the Church in the last days because of the example of its women.[1]

The point is, there are many passages like Micah 4:13 that are often overlooked because the language is difficult or because one must be familiar with ancient traditions, poetic devices, histories, etc. in order to get at the full meaning. But such passages yield a many-layered richness to any who expend an effort to explore the possible meanings.

27

An "iron horn" was given to a king to celebrate a victory won in battle. Here it seems to mean that the Lord will give success.

"Threshing" or "harvesting" are nearly always symbols referring to missionary work.

Horses are shod so their feet will not wear down going over rough ground. Better than shoes, brass hoofs could never wear down—a symbol of promising endurance.

Arise and <u>thresh</u>, O daughter of Zion
for I will make thine <u>horn iron</u>
and I will make thy <u>hoofs brass</u>:
and thou shalt <u>beat in pieces</u> many people:
and I will <u>consecrate their gain unto the Lord</u>,
and their substance unto the Lord of the whole earth.

Another symbol referring to how grain was harvested. It means "harvest."

means to "solemnly give this harvest to the Lord."

STEP #7
DON'T UNDERESTIMATE
THE VALUE OF GENERAL INFORMATION

Descriptions of how women dressed, where they lived (Ezekiel's wife built a mud-brick hut on the banks of a canal), the festivals they enjoyed (the Feast of the Tabernacles required women to construct arbors of green boughs), their occupations (everything from dancers to diplomats), etc., can add interest to your reading. Some of the information can be fun. For example do you know what not to wear?

1. tinkling ornaments about your feet
2. chains, bracelets, and mufflers
3. round headdresses like the moon (whatever those are)
4. bonnets
5. leg ornaments
6. headbands
7. earrings
8. cauls
9. rings
10. nose jewels

28

In one place or another the scriptures prohibit all those forms of feminine attire. OK, I'll admit to wearing rings, earrings, chains, and bracelets. So why is this kind of information important? For one thing it illustrates the fact that God and his prophets have always expressed an interest in women being appropriately dressed. Inappropriate dress was often viewed as symptomatic of pride, haughtiness, the "stretched-forth necks" described in Isaiah—all among the attitudes least conducive to individual spiritual growth. However, the scriptures also indicate that notions of "appropriate dress" have always allowed for wide cultural and individual diversity; thus I'm allowed those bracelets, earrings, etc., not acceptable in other times and places.

General information helps enliven the reading, creating pictures of women doing everyday things. It helps us remember that women have always been delightfully diverse and at the same time remarkably similar in their needs and concerns whenever or wherever they have lived. The bonus is that general information can yield some surprising gems of insight. For example, the nameless groups of women that followed Jesus create a composite picture of the kind of women the Savior liked to have around him. I find that useful.

STEP #8
LAST BUT NOT LEAST,
READ WITH THE SPIRIT

First give thanks that you can read the scriptures. Throughout history few women have been literate, and even those who could read were often denied access to sacred texts. For example, the Talmud (a book of instructions sacred to the Jews) forbids teaching women scriptures, saying: "whoever teaches his daughter Torah is as though he taught her obscenity" (*Mishnah Sotah* 3, 4).

A true appreciation of what it means to be a woman living in the latter-days needs to begin with an understanding of the privilege it is to have scriptures. No other women, today or in times past, ever had the amount and diversity of scripture now available to Latter-day Saint women. Lydia (Acts 16:13-15) would have envied us. Living in the first century after Christ, she "constrained," or begged, the Apostle Paul to tarry in her home in Macedonia and teach her. It was the only means she had of learning, and she was a member of the wealthy, privileged class of her day.

Such appreciation can only aid in your quest for the Holy Spirit. Such a quest is a personal matter involving fasting, prayer and a strong desire to have the same Holy

Spirit attend your reading as attended the writing of the sacred texts. In the end, spiritual matters can be understood only by spiritual means. But be assured that no one who desires to understand will be denied that understanding. Your capacity to comprehend spiritual matters will be enlarged by spiritual means. God has promised it.

And that's my quick course in How to Read the Scriptures and Not Miss the Women. Now, go, read, enjoy.

> *Search the scriptures; for in them ye think ye have eternal life: and they are they which testify of me. (John 5:39)*

Note
[1] See *Ensign*, May 1978, p. 5–7.

THE PARABLES JESUS TAUGHT WOMEN

A couple of years ago, several women from a prominent center-city Protestant congregation in my area picketed their church's annual Easter Pageant. They wanted more roles for women in the play. The pastor and church board of directors, all men, went to the media looking for sympathetic support. "Jesus was a man," one member of the church board said into a broadcaster's microphone, "and the twelve apostles were all men. We can't change that!"

I followed that controversy for several weeks, enjoying a detached sense of amusement. I figured this was one the women were going to win. And I was right.

Before I get to the parables Jesus taught women, let me set the stage for our own discussion.

Women figure prominently in the life and mission of our Savior. The one who comes to mind first, I think, is his mother, Mary. She was told by the angel announcing the birth that she would be known as the most blessed of all women. But even before that announcement, she had been seen by prophets foretelling that event.

Isaiah saw her in a vision and Nephi saw her with the baby Jesus. King Benjamin foretold that her name would be Mary. Another interesting reference in the Book of Mormon concerns King Lamoni. After hearing the missionary Ammon, King Lamoni was overcome and lay unconscious for three days, caught up with the Spirit. When he awoke, he exclaimed his great joy at having seen his Savior. He had also seen the woman who would be the mother of Jesus and was particularly anxious to convey this fact to his wife. He seemed to think it was important that she know about this great woman (Alma 19:12–13).

Much more could be said about Mary, but besides being the "most blessed among women," she is one of three women who epitomize the close alliance women have always had with the unfolding purposes of God. They are: Eve, who brought sin into the world; Mary, who brought the Savior into the world; and Mary Magdalene, who was the first witness to the resurrected Christ.

We know the least about Mary Magdalene, who was given the great honor of being the first to see the risen Christ. She was a wealthy and influential woman from the town of Magdala who had been healed by Jesus. She had then become one of his closest associates, contributing her time and substance to the Savior's cause. But I have to assume Mary Magdalene's devotion was based on more than gratitude for being healed. The Savior healed many, including ten lepers, nine of whom didn't even return to thank him. Healing alone did not make converts, and while there is no account of how Mary Magdalene came to be converted—how she came to her knowledge of the gospel—she seems to have known who Jesus was.

The same can be said of the sisters Mary and Martha of Bethany, whose brother Lazarus was raised from the dead. I find these two women particularly interesting because of their diverse personalities.

Jesus was a guest in the home of Mary and Martha during the Feast of the Tabernacles one year—a particularly busy time for Jewish women, when a banquet needed to be prepared and arbors of green boughs constructed and decorated in observance of the holiday. On this particular occasion, not only Jesus but several of his followers were dining in Mary and Martha's home. That creates a set of circumstances sure to make even the most casual hostess begin to feel a little harried.

Martha was busy with the preparations. Her sister Mary sat at Jesus' feet listening to him. Martha, feeling more and more irritated, at last vented her feelings: "Lord dost thou not care that my sister hath left me to serve alone?" She could have simply asked her sister to come and help, but she was more annoyed than that. She wanted to involve the Savior in the argument by asking why he let Mary sit at his feet when he could see how hard she was working.

We all know his reply. It was gentle, but pointed: "Martha, Martha, thou art careful and troubled about many things: But one thing is needful: and Mary hath chosen that good part, which shall not be taken away from her" (Luke 10:38–42). The necessities of life, meals, laundry, the more mundane aspects of child-care, all these intrude upon our loftier goals at one time or another. While having the Savior justify balancing those tasks with spiritual pursuits provides comfort, does the Savior really mean that Mary, sitting at his feet, is more devoted than her sister Martha, who is fixing his dinner?

I like to point out that on another occasion the Savior healed Peter's mother-in-law so that she could get up and "minister unto them" (see Matt. 8:14-15). "Minister," in this instance, would be better translated as "waited at table."[1] On yet another occasion Christ turned water into wine for his mother so that guests at a wedding feast would not have to do without. To me, that suggests that in the Savior's mind those things were not unimportant. And then one must remember that it was to Martha that he declared, "I am the resurrection, and the life: he that believeth in me, though he were dead, yet shall he live" (John 11:25).

The story is well known (John 11). Mary and Martha's brother Lazarus had been dead for four days. He had been buried in a tomb. When Martha heard that Jesus was coming, she ran out to meet him, saying, "Lord, if thou hadst been here, my brother had not died." It would have been only natural as she struggled with her grief for that thought

33

to have manifest itself over and over: If only the Savior had been here.

But Martha hadn't given up hope. She added, "I know, that even now, whatsoever thou wilt ask of God, God will give it thee."

Jesus said, "Thy brother shall rise again."

She knew that. She believed in the Resurrection and replied, "I know that he will rise again."

This is when Jesus declared himself to be the resurrection and the life, adding, "Whosoever liveth and believeth in me shall never die. Believest thou this?"

Martha had not yet seen her brother called forth out of the tomb, but she believed in Jesus. Without hesitation, she said, "Yea, Lord: I believe that thou art the Christ, the Son of God, which should come into the world."

Only then did the Savior ask about Mary. Martha went to get her, saying, "The Master is come, and calleth for thee."

Mary ran weeping to fall at Jesus' feet.

To the practical Martha, Jesus declared himself the resurrection and the life. With the weeping Mary, he wept. Then he asked to be shown the sepulchre and after praying, giving thanks, and acknowledging the Father, he called Lazarus forth from the dead.

The point I want to make is that under differing circumstances in differing ways, the Savior acknowledged the testimonies of both Mary and Martha with no indication that he favored one above the other but with every indication that he understood their differences and appreciated them.

In addition to his mother, Mary Magdalene, and the sisters Mary and Martha, there were a number of women closely associated with the Savior who frequently traveled with him and his apostles. These included Peter's wife; another woman named Salome, who was the mother of

34

John the Revelator and James the Younger; Mary the wife of Cleophas; Susanna; Joanna; Mary, the mother of John Mark; and others.

These were all active women, knowledgeable about the affairs of their day, who enjoyed some prominence in their communities. Mary, the mother of John Mark, is a typical example. Her son wrote the Gospel of Mark, and she owned a house in Jerusalem with a large upper chamber which the Savior frequently used as a meeting place.

Women Who Traveled with Jesus

PETER'S WIFE
  Matt. 8:14–15; Mark 1:30–31; Luke 4:38–39; 1 Cor. 9:5

SALOME
  Matt.20:20–21; 27:56; Mark 16:1–8

MARY, Wife of Cleophas
  Matt. 27:56–61; Mark 15:40; 16:1; Luke 24:10; John 19:25

SUSANNA
  Luke 8:2–3

JOANNA
  Luke 8:3; 24:10

MARY, MOTHER of JOHN MARK
  Acts 12:12–13; Rom. 16:3–5; 1 Cor. 16:19; 2 Tim. 4:19

All these women had free and easy access to the Savior. He sought them out, enjoyed their company, and seemed to have considered them close friends. He discussed his mission with them, taught them, and commissioned various of them with specific tasks or assignments, including admonishing them to carry his message to others. They, in turn, supported him and his work with both their means and their personal efforts. We don't know a great deal about these women, but we know as much or more about them as we do about the minor apostles. The scriptures are brief accounts at best. But taken together these women illustrate both the number and the variety of women Jesus gathered around himself. I find that useful—knowing the kind of women Jesus enjoyed associating with.

In addition to the women who were closely associated with him, the Savior interacted with a great number of women—healing them or teaching them or in some other manner significantly affecting their lives through some encounter with him. Gathering this data creates a picture of just how many women were part of Jesus' life.

Of course, Jesus was a man and his twelve original apostles were men, as the Protestant church board member pointed out in the midst of the controversy surrounding his congregation's Easter pageant. But women surrounded the Savior, too. They were part of his everyday life and deeply involved in his work. A Passion play needs to reflect that fact to be accurate. We need to picture it in our own minds to really understand. Once we grasp that view, it will seem natural to also notice that as he taught, using parables, Jesus told many stories that involved women as the main characters and included experiences that women could readily relate to their own activities. Surely he was speaking to the women around him.

The incident I think illustrates better than any other the Savior's sensitivity to things uniquely feminine has to do with the woman who had a twelve-year issue of blood. According to Jewish law, any blood that issued from the female organ was considered "unclean." A woman who had given birth went through a ritual cleansing. During her monthly cycle, a woman would be considered unclean for a number of days until she bathed and went through a similar ritual cleansing. During those times when she was unclean, a woman was forbidden to touch a Jewish man because if he were to be touched by such a woman, he would be made unclean and would have to go through a cleansing ritual. In this case, a woman with some abnormality had suffered a twelve-year issue of blood—for twelve years she had been unclean, unable to touch a man or participate in religious services or function in many other aspects of normal Jewish life. That was in addition to whatever weakness or disability the condition caused her physically. But this woman, by her own faith, came to believe she would be healed if she could but touch the hem of the Savior's garment.

We are all familiar with the story (Mark 5:23–43). Jesus was on his way to heal Jairus's daughter, and there was a huge crowd around him thronging him on every side. Suddenly he stopped and asked, "Who touched me?"

Peter, pointing out the obvious—the crowd all around—asked what Christ meant by the words "Who touched me?"

Note that the Savior did not say that he suddenly felt "unclean." He noted, rather, that "virtue [or healing power] had gone out of him."

Realizing that she had been discovered, the woman threw herself at Jesus' feet and confessed. Confessed? What did she have to confess? That she had touched a Jewish man in her "unclean" condition. But Jesus didn't even mention that. He didn't leave the crowd and go off to the baths. Instead he acknowledged her courage and strong belief saying, "Daughter . . . thy faith hath made thee whole."

Then he continued on to Jairus's house, even though he had been told that the young girl was already dead. Jewish law also stated that touching a dead body made one "unclean." Again, Jesus disregarded that prohibition. He took the girl by her hand and using a Hebrew phrase that might be translated "little lambkins come" (v. 41), he told her to arise.

These are not isolated examples. Consider the sensitivity with which he handled the adulterous woman. As you remember, the scribes and Pharisees brought the Savior a woman who had been taken in adultery. They intended to use the situation as a means of entrapping him. If Jesus said the woman should be stoned, they would accuse him before the Romans, who did not allow the Jews to carry out capital punishment. However, if he said she should not be stoned, they could accuse him before the church officials for not upholding the Mosaic Law. In setting up this situation, it is clear the scribes and Pharisees had no particular concern for the woman, except for how they could use her for their own purposes. At the same time, the Savior had reason to be concerned about himself. If the scribes and Pharisees were successful in their accusations . . . If they could turn the opinion of the crowds following him . . . The situation clearly had an element of real personal danger. Yet Jesus focused on the woman, taking particular care for her feelings.

He stooped and with his finger wrote on the ground as if he hadn't heard the question. When the scribes and Pharisees asked him again, he said, "He that is without sin among you, let him first cast a stone at her" (John 8:7). Then he continued to write on the ground until, looking up, he saw there was no one left but the woman. At that moment, I imagine both Jesus and the woman were aware of her guilt. She had been taken in the very act of adultery. But with great kindness and a recognition of the shame she had already suffered, he simply admonished her to go and sin no more.

That was a teaching moment. The Savior used or created many such moments. In fact Jesus gave parable after parable until another teacher might have exhausted his store of knowledge, but not the Master. He went on, fresh and interesting, finding lessons and shadows of the kingdom in everything. That meant his students could do the same. They could contemplate the kingdom as they worked, doing ordinary things like sowing seeds or making bread.

Jesus taught that the kingdom of God is like a mustard seed that a man took and sowed in his field. From this, the smallest of all seeds, a tree grew large enough to lodge birds. He paused. He asked, "Now what shall I liken the kingdom of God to?" Then he said, "The kingdom of God is like unto leaven which a woman took and hid [or added] in three measures of meal, till the whole was leavened" (Matt. 13:33).

That balance of paired stories that relate to a man's experience (sewing mustard seeds in a field) and a woman's experience (working leaven into a lump of dough) is typical of the Savior's teachings. Luke especially preserves the parallel. In Luke, Jesus speaks of the many widows at the time of Elias, none of whom received the prophet, except one, and of the many lepers at the time of Eliseus, none of whom came to the prophet to be cured, except one (4:25–27). He compares the Ninevites who listened to Jonah to the Queen of Sheba who came from the farthermost parts of the earth to hear Solomon (Luke 11:30–32). He describes men in fields and women at grindstones.

Scattered through the rest of the Gospels are stories of the shepherd's lost sheep and the woman's lost coin; the neighbor asked to give bread for an unexpected guest and the judge asked to give judgment for a persistent widow; the servants and their talents and the virgins and their oil. The care with which Jesus provides stories and images that hearken to the experiences of both sexes has to be deliberate.

His actions were often similarly balanced. In the twelfth chapter of Luke, Jesus is shown teaching a man, answering his question with the parable of the good Samaritan. Immediately following that, he enters Mary and Martha's house and encourages Mary to sit at his feet and learn. Later he heals first a woman and then a man on the Sabbath (Luke 13:10–16 and 14:2–6). Then he healed a Gentile's daughter, followed by a deaf man (Mark 7:24–30 and 31–37). Still later, he healed a woman, raised Jairus's daughter from the dead, and then healed two blind men (Matt. 9:20–22, 23–26, and 27–34). Another time he healed the centurion's servant and immediately afterward raised the widow of Nain's son.

At times Jesus described himself using feminine images: "If any man thirst, let him come unto me, and drink," or "nurse" as some translators render it (John 37:7); and "How often would I have gathered thy children together as a hen doth gather her brood under her wings." (Matt. 23:37; Luke 13:34). Using feminine descriptions in this way was something his contemporary rabbis would never have done. In fact, tradition was for a man to speak to a woman only through her father or husband. A widow spoke through her son. Jesus is never shown doing that. He speaks directly to women, inviting them to respond directly. There is no intermediary.[2]

Jesus' manner of teaching was remarkable in its break from tradition. Also remarkable is the fact that his parallel parables build on one another with little redundancy. For example the mustard seed that the man sows in his field grows into a tree and expands its branches until a solid structure has been built. The leaven, or yeast, the wise woman works into her bread dough disseminates and diffuses through the mass. Both understandings are true of God's kingdom and how it will be established. Both images are necessary to contemplate the whole.

Likewise the shepherd searching for his lost sheep and the woman searching for her lost coin both illustrate the joy of heaven over one sinner returned (Luke 15). In the first story, a shepherd leaves his ninety and nine sheep to search for a lost lamb. In the second story, a woman having lost a coin sweeps and cleans her house until she finds it again. Similar stories, but the differences are also notable. The lost lamb wandered off on its own. The coin was lost because of carelessness. The shepherd regains his sheep and returns joyfully to the village. The woman finds her coin and looks around to discover that the dusty corners and dirty recesses of her house have, in the process of her search, become clean. Again both understandings are true of how the lost must be found. Both kind of searches need to be undertaken.

Perhaps more significant than the number or balance of images is the quality of the female examples found in the gospels. Consistently in his stories, Jesus presents pictures of strong women acting positively in their own behalf. Even the parable of the widow who seeks a judgment, which has been characterized by some Bible commentators as "the story of an obnoxious nag," is told matter-of-factly by Jesus as an example of how one ought to pray.

He tells it this way (Luke 18:1–8): There was a judge in a certain city who "feared not God, neither regarded man." Those are Jesus' words—his description of the judge. One day a widow came before this judge seeking justice for some wrong done her. The judge, seeing no personal advantage in giving her a judgment, delayed acting on her behalf. But the woman came repeatedly before him pleading her case until he said to himself, "yet because this widow troubleth me, I will avenge her, lest by her continual coming she weary me."

The story doesn't imply that the widow was seeking favors. She does not play games to win the judge's sympathy or to make herself attractive to him. Rather, she repeatedly states her position, her right under the law, indicating she was not uninformed. If she knew the judge was uncomfortable about her case and her presence before him, she did not make it easy for him. And how did she finally win her case? Not on its merits. The judge found it convenient to decide in her favor.

How can this be a metaphor for prayer? Assuming the

judge represents God, can God be swayed by persistence?

Luke's companion parable, told from masculine point of view, portrays a man who, finding at midnight that he must feed an unexpected guest, goes to his friend and neighbor, and asks for three loaves of bread. His friend, though the hour is late and his children are in bed and his house is locked up, does not long refuse the request. He arises and gives what is needed. Jesus follows this story with the admonition: "Ask, and it shall be given you; Seek, and ye shall find; knock, and it shall be opened unto you" (Luke 11:5–9).

At the end of the parable of the widow seeking a judgment, the Savior admonishes his followers to pray always, the implication being that women and men alike should approach their God directly and often with all of their concerns. If an unrighteous judge can be moved by continual pleading, how much more so our Heavenly Father who wants to hear and answer our prayers?

Jesus frequently spoke of widows. During the Passover week, he noticed a widow adding her two small coins to the offerings and said, "Of a truth I say unto you, that this poor widow hath cast in more than they all" (Luke 21:3).

How can that be? How can two mites, hardly enough to buy a loaf of bread, be more than all the other offerings left at the temple during that holiday week? Because it was the widow's willing spirit that was measured out for her that day and made into an object lesson that Jesus wanted his other followers to notice.

On another occasion, Jesus called a child to him, and sitting the child in the midst of his followers, he told them that they must humble themselves as a little child, for the same was the greatest in the kingdom of God. He added that whosoever received a little child, received him. He capped that lesson with a warning—that whosoever offended a little child offended God and that it were better for a millstone to be hanged around that person's neck and that they be drowned in the sea than to be guilty of such an offense. Strong words!

One day Jesus was approached by a number of people who brought their children. His apostles seemed to think they might be troublesome to their master. But Jesus stopped and called them and their little ones to him saying, "Suffer the little children to come unto me, and forbid them not: for of such is the kingdom of God" (Mark 10:14).

That calling of the little children was repeated and magnified on the American continent. When Jesus came to visit the Nephites, he commanded that the little ones be brought to him. The scriptures describe the multitudes parting, giving way, that the children might come forward. Then when the children were all gathered around him, Jesus knelt in their midst and asked the multitude to kneel with them. Then Jesus prayed, and the scriptures say that "the things which he prayed cannot be written. . . . The eye hath never seen, neither hath the ear heard, before, so great and marvelous things as . . . Jesus [spoke] unto the Father" (3 Ne. 17:15–16).

The multitude was overcome with joy. Jesus arose, wept, and blessed the children, praying to the Father for them. When he had finished, he wept again. Then, turning to the multitude, Jesus said, "Behold, your little ones." The multitude looked and saw the heavens open; angels descended and encircled the children as if with fire, ministering to the little ones. According to the Apostle Nephi, the multitude numbered two thousand five hundred souls, men, women and children. All saw and all bore record of that wondrous event.

On a subsequent visit to the Nephites, Jesus loosened the tongues of the children and they spoke what is described in scripture as "great and marvelous things" (3 Ne. 26:14). Even the babies opened their mouths and uttered things so wondrous, that Nephi was forbidden to record them. Jesus explained that he was showing greater things to the Nephites than anything he had shown the Jews because their faith was greater. Some of these things he showed through their children.

In all his teachings, Jesus used powerful examples. He created precise pictures of birthing and babies and children and leaven and sweeping out one's house. His language, full of both masculine and feminine images, was meant to teach and illustrate and at the same time touch those feelings both men and women hold most dear.

My favorite parable, because it looks forward to my own time, is the parable of the ten virgins. The story is based on marriage customs familiar to Jesus' followers but which require some explanation today. Among the wealthier classes in Jesus' time, it was fashionable for the bridegroom to celebrate with his friends and relatives at his home and for the bride to do the same at her home until sometime after dark, when the bridegroom would lead a torchlight procession through the streets of the village on his way to the bride's house where he would join her in a celebration that culminated in an enormous wedding feast. Villagers who wished to witness the marriage and take part in the feast would watch and join the bridegroom's procession as it passed by, adding their lamps, usually attached to the end of a rod, to the brilliancy and beauty of the bridegroom's procession.

In Jesus' story, ten maids, called virgins, wait for the bridegroom's party, hoping to be among his well-wishers at the feast. But the bridegroom is unusually late. It is not only after dark, it is near midnight. Five of the maids have not prepared for such an eventuality. Awakened by the fore-runners of the marriage party, they discover that their lamps have gone out. Unable to buy or borrow oil at such a late hour, they are refused admission to the marriage feast. Their wiser sisters, ready with extra oil, are invited to enter.

Whom does Jesus hope will be prepared and waiting at his Second Coming? Kings? Priests? Officials? Yes, of course! He wants and hopes everyone will be prepared and waiting for him. But for me, there is special meaning in the fact that for his story Jesus singled out a few women carrying their own lamps—lit with their own oil.

Wherever he went, Jesus encouraged women to develop their own light—their own spirituality. Returning to Galilee from Jerusalem one time, he took the unpopular road through Samaria and stopped to rest near Jacob's Well (John 4:1–30). A woman came to the well with her pitcher, and Jesus asked her for a drink of water. She was a woman who had lived a worldly life, having been passed from man to man, and she was immediately suspicious that he should so boldly address her. She asked, "How is it that thou, being a Jew, askest drink of me, which am a woman of Samaria?"

Jesus replied, "If thou knewest . . . who it is that saith to thee, Give me to drink; thou wouldest have asked of him living water."

Surprising words, but the woman looked at Jesus, and it was obvious he didn't have a pitcher or a bucket or anything with which to draw water and she knew Jacob's well was deep. I visited Jacob's Well once and discovered for myself how deep it is. I was invited to pour a cup of water down that well. I did and set the cup back down and then counted, one, two, three . . . Only then did I hear the water splash at the bottom. That is a deep well, and this woman came regularly to draw her water there, so knowing how hard it is to pull water up from that depth, she asked Jesus, "From whence then has thou that living water?"

Jesus pointed to the well and replied, "Whosoever drinketh of this water shall thirst again: But whosoever drinketh of the water that I shall give him shall never thirst."

The woman, failing to understand, replied, "Sir, give me this water, that I thirst not, nor come hither to draw."

Jesus cut her short. "Go, call thy husband, and come hither."

Why did the Savior suddenly command in that manner? Was he resorting to proper protocol—seeking to address her only through her husband? As I pointed out earlier, some of the more pious Jews of his day believed that women should only be addressed through their husband or father— never directly. But Jesus had never followed that tradition before, so why now?

On the other hand, he knew the woman's situation. Was he trying to embarrass her?

The answer may be found in the woman's response.

"I have no husband," said the woman of Samaria, and having confessed, she became a different woman—her hardness, her mocking attitude changed. Jesus had asked the question closest to her heart, the question that humbled and made her teachable. With her past revealed, what could she answer? She said, "Sir, I perceive that thou art a prophet."

Then in that marvelous way in which Jesus taught all who were teachable, he filled her soul like water flowing into a jar. She asked him several questions, and he answered them. Something about his answers seems to have made her wonder who he was.

She commented, "I know that Messias cometh, which is called Christ: when he is come, he will tell us all things."

Jesus declared to her, "I . . . am he."

Jesus made his first recorded declaration of his divine Sonship to a Samaritan woman who was living with a man who was not her husband. He quickened the spirit of this worldly woman. She drank of his "living water" and was spiritually refreshed. Having partaken, the power she carried away with her from the Master's presence was enough to inspire her whole village.

Many of the parables Jesus taught women
are mentioned again in the Doctrine and Covenants:
D&C 10:65; 29:2; 43:24; 101:81–84; 109:74

The parable of the virgins and their oil
is mentioned repeatedly:
D&C 33:17; 45:56; 63:54

Does Jesus expect the same of women today?

The Doctrine and Covenants has been described as the scripture most addressed to this age. But the Doctrine and Covenants is unique among the scriptures in that it contains few references to women and no stories. Made up of a collection of revelations given to Joseph Smith and others, it consists mainly of instructions, but also contains warnings, commandments and repeated references to the parables Jesus taught women: the parable of the widow seeking a judgment, the parable of the hen gathering her chicks, the parable of the ten virgins . . .

That is entirely within character—a reflection of the way Jesus has always taught.

47

Notes

1   J.R. Dummelow, ed., *A Commentary on the Holy Bible by Various Writers* (1936; reprint, New York: Macmillan Publishing Co., Inc., 1989).

2   Leonard Swidler, *The Biblical Affirmations of Women* (Philadelphia: The Westminster Press, 1979), p. 163–64.

THE SCRIPTURES AND THE
SINGLE WOMAN

The phone rings in my house, I answer, and it is a Relief Society President from a stake in Pennsylvania, Virginia, or maybe New Jersey. She is planning a special woman's meeting and she wants to know if I'll be one of the speakers.

Seldom in these telephone conversations do we discuss in any detail what I'll talk about. I really have only one subject: the women found in scripture. Often I adapt my comments to fit a particular theme. Or I may speak using different titles and varied examples, but in one way or another I always discuss my sisters in the scriptures and how a knowledge of their examples can strengthen women today and why a woman might want to seek that strength.

Knowing that, I'm surprised by the next question. More often than not, I am asked: "Do you have something you could address specifically to the single sisters?"

How do you answer that? I think everything I say is addressed to single sisters and married sisters, tall sisters and short sisters, to all my sisters, black or brown, brunette or blond. There are no sisters so unique by circumstance or personal characteristic that they cannot be strengthened by a knowledge of the womanly examples found in scripture.

For years I explained that my material applied equally to all sisters, and I would be unable to offer anything focused on singles.

So why did I change my mind?

The phone rang at my house. On the other end was a Unitarian minister—a woman. She was putting together a workshop on women and religion and wanted to know if I would participate representing Mormon women. I explained to her that I had no official capacity as a representative of my church. I was simply a member. I suggested she contact the mission president in my area.

She didn't want to do that. I had written two books on the subject of women and the scriptures, including the Mormon scriptures, and she felt this gave me the expertise she wanted. I assured her that I did feel I had something to share and that I spoke fairly often, but always informally, always as the guest of whomever had asked me. And because I thought she would be interested, I added that more often than not, when I'm asked to speak, I am asked by a woman.

She was intrigued that there was a vehicle for such expression within the Mormon church—a way for women to talk to other women. And being intrigued, she asked if I would meet and talk with her at greater length.

I found her to be pleasant, committed, intellectually stimulating, and very much at peace with herself. I don't know what I gave her; I hope I improved her notion of Mormon women. She seemed to think we were uninformed and largely nonparticipants in our own religious experience. But she gave me an important insight into why I was being asked over and over again to "say something to the single sisters."

We discussed a wide range of topics. I was interested in the research she was doing and what she was trying to accomplish with her workshops on women and religion. She was interested in several aspects of what I was doing, but returned repeatedly to a particular line of questions: What did women want to know? What kind of questions did women ask me? What concerns did the women I was meeting express? I sensed that her interest stemmed from a strongly held belief that traditional religion was not satisfying women in some fundamental way.

I had to think. I do field a lot of questions when I speak. The questions vary, yet without thinking too hard, I realized there was a theme to the things I am most often asked.

A single sister wanted to know if there would be single men available in the next life. And how many did I think there would be? She didn't want to be someone's second wife. She'd waited, refusing to settle for second best. She didn't want to think she was going to have to settle for second anything in eternity.

A woman married to a man who was living unworthy of their temple vows felt uncomfortable with the notion that she might be given to someone else in the next life. She laughed and said she ought to take up smoking, too, but she was half-serious. She loved her husband despite his faults and wanted to know what I thought about her situation.

I find it difficult to respond to these kinds of issues.

And I found it difficult to explain them to that Unitarian minister. I felt I had to tell her about temple marriage and the three degrees of glory and the distinction we Mormons make between merely going to heaven and being exalted to become like gods and goddesses. Midway through my rambling, she sat back and shook her head.

"Those questions have nothing to do with your doctrines about marriage and eternity," she said. "The women want to know if their feelings matter. It's the same question women are asking everywhere."

The women want to know if their feelings matter.

Of course.

And in the same instant I understood why I was getting repeated requests to "say something to the single sisters." All women worry about their feelings. No one likes to think her feelings might be ignored, discounted or cast aside. None of us can contemplate with any ease being asked to do something contrary to our deepest desires. What's more, we can't afford it. Any time a person acts contrary to her heart-felt feelings, the cost will bankrupt her spiritually.

And that's not what the gospel of Jesus Christ teaches. Jesus startled many of his followers when he taught that how one feels matters as much as what one does.

"Ye have heard that it was said by them of old time, Thou shalt not kill; and whosoever shall kill shall be in danger of the judgment: But I say unto you, that whosoever is angry with his brother without a cause shall be in danger of the judgment" (Matt. 5:21–22).

"Ye have heard that it was said by them of old time, Thou shalt not commit adultery: But I say unto you, that whosoever looketh on a woman to lust after her hath committed adultery with her already in his heart" (Matt. 5:27–28).

In other words, we will be judged by the righteous desires of our hearts, not some outward, observable characteristic. Our true judge, our Savior, who knows our hearts, will reward accordingly with all the joys of heaven. Knowing that, it is unthinkable to suggest he would reward a faithful sister with something she not only does not desire, but considers an anathema.

The restored gospel's teachings on eternal marriage and the joy of living eternally with a beloved companion should never be cheapened with a hint that some sister "ought" to ignore her feelings and settle for a less than desirable companion simply because she "needs" to be married in the temple. No one who fully understands the gospel can suggest that a woman will receive a lesser reward simply because she doesn't marry, or that she will be "given" to a righteous man in the next life, implying little choice on her part. It doesn't work that way because her feelings do matter.

But because of our particular emphasis on eternal marriage being a requirement for exaltation, we sometimes create anxiety among those who have not yet participated in that sacred ordinance. As a result, the question of whether or not our feelings matter tends to be framed in terms of marriage perplexities and asked largely by single women—almost as if they were speaking for all of us.

I'm not the only one hearing those questions. Nor am I the only one who feels unequal to answering them. And so it may be that Relief Society leaders all over the Church, sensing the urgency of the concerns behind such questions, have come to the conclusion that single women need special assurance.

"We've got to provide something for our single sisters," I hear over my telephone.

Single or not, we women need to reassure each another. And I started agreeing to "say something to the single sisters" when it occurred to me that single sisters might best be able to start that process by reassuring their leaders that feelings matter—not only to us but to our Righteous Judge. Consider the story of Elijah and the widow of Zarephath (1 Kgs. 17).

Elijah, as you will remember from your Old Testament studies, was the great prophet who opposed the wicked King Ahab and Queen Jezebel. When the wickedness of this king and queen and their followers threatened to take over the whole country, Elijah sealed the heavens. No rain fell for three years—none at all—not even a sprinkle. This caused a terrible famine. King Ahab and Queen Jezebel suspected that Elijah was behind the calamity, but rather than repent, they wanted to kill the prophet. So Elijah had to flee. For a long time he hid in the wilderness and was fed by ravens, but then the drought became so severe that the brook near his cave dried up, and the prophet Elijah needed to find some other haven.

Caught in the middle of this was a widow living in the town of Zarephath with her one son. As the famine became more and more severe, she found herself with fewer and fewer resources. Finally one day she went outside the city wall to gather a few sticks. She planned to build a fire and cook the last bit of her meal and oil. Then she expected that she and her son would die of starvation.

As she was gathering those sticks, she was approached by the prophet. But she didn't know him. He was from another country. She recognized from his accent that he was a Jew, and the people of her country despised the Jews. Nevertheless, she also noted that he was dusty and travel weary.

He asked her for a drink of water.

She didn't snap back, "Go get the water yourself, I have my own problems to worry about." No. She could see he was thirsty and she could get him water, so she did. The stranger then asked her for some food.

She hesitated. She explained that she had only enough food for one final meal for herself and her son. Elijah assured her not to worry, but to fix him a little cake anyway. Still she didn't know that he was a prophet, though he did promise in the name of the God of Israel that if she were to make him a cake first, she and her son would not go without food. It wouldn't be until much later when he raised her son from the dead that she would know and acknowledge that he was a man of God. At this point, all she could see was that he was hungry. She had a little food. He had none. But something must have stirred her faith, and she invited him to share her last meal with her and her son. And miraculously, her meal and oil multiplied itself so that each day there was just enough for yet another meal, and each day she shared it with Elijah.

The little bit of meal and oil that the widow of Zarephath shared with Elijah was small next to her willing spirit. I am sure she was blessed not only for what she gave, but for the generous feelings that she expressed, for the way she was able to recognize a need in someone else even as she faced her own uncertain future.

The earth and everything in it belongs to the Lord. He could have found another way to feed Elijah. Instead, the Lord gave this woman a chance to express her faith and her generosity. And then he blessed her for it. He didn't suddenly fill her coffers and make all her problems disappear over night. But he was with her, always with her, every day. In Isaiah, the Lord states that it would be easier for a mother to forget her suckling child than for him to forget us.

Let me give you another example of a single woman who gave all she had to the Church, didn't get immediate blessings, and yet never regretted her sacrifice nor lost faith.

If you'll look in the 90th section of the Doctrine and Covenants you'll notice the 28th verse speaks of a woman called Vienna Jaques. The 90th section doesn't say much about this woman, but I want to tell you her story.[1] She was a single woman who had never married. She was working as a nurse in Boston when she heard about Joseph Smith. She got a copy of the Book of Mormon, read it, and through her own study and prayer became convinced that the book was true and Joseph Smith must be a modern prophet. She wanted to meet him.

Vienna Jaques was not a young woman. She was the same age as Joseph Smith's mother, and for a woman of middle age to travel alone from Boston to Kirtland, Ohio, in those days was a major undertaking, but she went. She met the Prophet, was baptized, and wanted to join the Saints in Ohio, so she went back to Boston, concluded her affairs and gathered all her worldly wealth—about $2400—and returned to Kirtland. When she arrived, Joseph Smith asked her to give all her money to the Church and go to Missouri.

Here was a woman who had no one to rely on but herself, and she was getting older. The Prophet was asking her to give up her security—her nest egg put away for her old age—and worse, he was asking her, a single woman, to go and live on the frontier. Missouri was considered a wild wilderness at that time. But Joseph Smith went on to promise this woman that if she made this offering, she would find peace and prosperity in "the land of Zion."

Vienna Jaques gave all her worldly wealth to the Church, and as is stated in the Doctrine and Covenants section 90, the Church gave her back enough of her money to make the trip to Missouri. But like the other Saints who went to Missouri, she did not find peace or prosperity there.

When Joseph Smith arrived with Zion's Camp, he found Vienna Jaques among the members of the Church who had been driven out of their homes. But even when she had no shelter of her own, when the members of Zion's Camp were stricken with cholera, it was Vienna Jaques who nursed the sick.

When Joseph Smith returned to Kirtland, he wrote Vienna Jaques a long letter. He seemed to have felt that he owed her some kind of explanation as to why she had not received the blessings she had been promised when she made her offering. But in his letter, Joseph Smith was careful to note that Vienna Jaques had not asked him for such an explanation. She didn't doubt he was a prophet. What she had expressed was a concern that her offering might not have been acceptable. Take note of that. She was not worried about the fact that she hadn't received all the blessings she had been promised. She was worried that maybe she hadn't given her money with the right spirit—that maybe her feelings hadn't been right; maybe she hadn't shown the Lord enough willing contriteness or gratitude. That was her concern because she knew that it was the feeling, the spirit, with which she had made her sacrifice that mattered more than what she had given.

Joseph assured her that her offering was acceptable to the Lord and that eventually she would see the Saints at peace.

Vienna Jaques married briefly while she was in Missouri, but the marriage was not happy. She later separated from her husband, and he cut her off in his will with a dollar and twenty-five cents. Nevertheless, she was one of the first women to arrive in the Salt Lake Valley in 1847, having driven her own wagon across the plains at age sixty. She lived to be ninety-six years old and finally saw the Saints settled peacefully in that valley.

There isn't anything any of us can offer the Lord that isn't his already—except our willing service and gratitude, our contrite hearts, our love and devotion. By the same token we are none of us so poor or so oppressed that we can't give him these, and richly.

One time Jesus made an object lesson of a widow and her two small coins. This woman entered the court of the temple, where he was teaching, to cast in her offering—her two mites, hardly enough to buy a loaf of bread. Streams of visitors were in the Holy City for the feast. Many of them were rich and were bringing huge offerings to the temple. The woman probably hoped to pass unnoticed that day, that the size of her meager contribution might not cause remark. But Jesus saw. He turned to his disciples and said, "Verily, I say unto you, That this poor widow hath cast more in than [they] all" (Mark 12:43).

Secular finance is money, nothing more. I don't know about your tax collector, but mine cares not a whit how I feel about paying my taxes, only that I pay and pay promptly. But tithing is different. From the Lord's view, our feelings, the spirit with which we give it, is all important.

Yet this widow went her way without ever knowing who watched her or what he said of her. She didn't need to know. It was for the benefit of his other followers that the Savior pointed out her example.

And the scriptures are rich with those kinds of examples of single sisters drawing upon their truest feelings in ways that are able to uplift all who learn of them, two and even three thousand years later. Returning to my usual theme, let me emphasize that I think women, all women, need to know about their sisters in the scriptures precisely because of the quality of the examples offered there. We need to be assured that what we value—our feelings and our relationships—are what the Lord and the prophets have always valued.

Also in the New Testament we learn of a widow whose work was so vital she was raised from the dead to continue her service. Her name was Dorcus. She lived in Joppa, a port city thirty-four miles northwest of Jerusalem. It was shortly after the death of the Savior, when the apostles were presiding over the Church and preaching the message of Christianity to all who would listen. Dorcus was a convert and she seems to be one of the women whose homes had become a gathering place for others who believed in Christ. More than that, she had turned her home into a refuge for the poor and was known throughout her city for the clothing she had sewn with her own hands and given to those who had no clothing.

57

Then one day she became ill and died. The others she had been helping, mostly widows and their children, were grief stricken. They sent for Peter who was preaching in a nearby town. When he came, they displayed for him all the coats and other garments that Dorcus had made and given them. They wanted to impress the apostle with the goodness of this woman, their friend. Peter was moved. He asked everyone to leave the room. Then he knelt and prayed. Using the Aramaic form of her name, "Tabitha," he called Dorcus forth from the dead, and she arose. Then with great rejoicing, Peter presented her to the other widows, alive. And the scriptures add that because of this miracle, many believed (Acts 9:36–42).

Dorcus's story sounds unique, but it isn't. What Dorcus was doing by opening her home and allowing her house to become the center of Christian activity in her city was being done by other women all over the Mediterranean area where the early apostles were preaching. Paul, especially, praises his women converts and credits them with aiding his work. "I commend unto you Phebe, our sister," he wrote, "for she hath been a succourer of many, and of myself also" (Rom. 16:2). He added, "Greet Mary, who bestowed much labour on us" (Rom. 16:6). "Salute Tryphena and Tryphosa who labour in the Lord. Salute the beloved Persis" (Rom. 16:12).

The pattern was for Paul to go into an area, preach the gospel, organize the converts into a small branch, and then leave to carry the message to yet another city. Often he would not be able to return for two or three years. But when he did, he would find that the women who had opened their homes to their fellow Christians had in the process nurtured those little congregations and helped them to grow and become stronger.

In Philemon the Christian church began with the baptism of the businesswoman Lydia and all her household (Acts 16:14–40). Her home then became a center of Christian missionary work, a place where Paul often preached and stayed. Other missionaries, including Barnabas and Apollos, also used the homes of Christian patronesses. Apphia opened her home in Colossae (Philem. 2). In Romans Paul praises Phebe, Mary, Tryphena, Tryphosa, Persis, and Julia (Rom. 16). He wrote his first letter to the Corinthians because of an inquiry from certain persons from the household of a woman named Chloe (1 Cor. 1:11). These women were all single.

You may not have been aware of that because the scriptures don't exactly say they were single women. That is the way it should be. A woman's age or marital status has no bearing on the service she can give. We have too many labels as it is. When we go around talking about "single sisters" or "special interests" or "Molly Mormons," those labels can separate us. We need inclusion, not exclusion. On the other hand, if we're going to reassure each other and be able to point out the womanly examples in scripture, there may be times when it can be helpful to know that these were single women, many of them older single women.

How do we know that? Because they are listed as heads of households, and scholars agree that no married woman would have been named in connection with her place of residence. Unless she were single, we would read about her husband's house and her husband's servants, even if he were not a Christian and she was.

I encourage all sisters to know the scriptures for themselves, especially the womanly examples found there. As you study, you will also discover that prophetic utterances concerning the coming Millenial rein of our Lord Jesus Christ tend to use female imagery such as "the Lamb's Bride," or "the Daughter of Zion." The Savior himself spoke of his first coming using the image of twelve fishermen and his second coming using the image of ten virgins. As Latter-day Saint women looking forward to that great coming event, I feel a particular urgency to read, to study, to desire a fuller knowledge. And I encourage anyone who will listen to do the same. The time has come when we must fill our lamps, light them, and wait, watching for him.

And our own peculiar personal circumstances—whether we are married or single, rich or poor, fat or thin—have nothing to do with our ability to get the light we need. Such illumination is equally available to all.

I had someone point out to me once that no divorcees were named in scripture. She seemed to feel that indicated a particular stigma. Not so. The term widow seems to have covered everything—even women who never married. But there have always been divorces. The ritual that Abraham went through when he cast off Hagar and sent her into the desert was a divorce. It was meant to show that Abraham no longer considered her or her son part of his household. It was meant to prevent their making any claim on him for

59

inheritance.

And it doesn't take much to recognize that Hagar was treated with great unfairness. She was a slave who was used and when she was no longer useful, she was cast off. But she was not cast off by the Lord. He sent her angels on more than one occasion and repeatedly pronounced blessings on her and her posterity.

Divorce laws in general as they are outlined in the Old and New Testaments are unfair. There were only two circumstances under which a man could not divorce his wife: if he had falsely accused her of not being a virgin when he married her, or if he married her because they were guilty of fornication. Otherwise he had only to send her home to her father (Deut. 23:19, 29; 24:1–5). But a woman had no divorce rights. She could not even claim support from her former husband. Nor did widows inherit from their dead husbands. They were left to rely on the charity of their sons, and if they had no sons, on their other kinspeople. Why, you might ask, did the Lord allow injustices like that? Why does he allow continued injustices?

That is one of the great questions philosophers have struggled over for centuries. The answer clearly lies in the Lord's firm, unwavering commitment to honor agency. The

Book of Mormon Prophets warned that the welfare of their nation hinged on the treatment of widows and fatherless:	*Others saw it that way too:*
2 Nephi 20:1–2	D&C 136:8
Mosiah 21:16–17	1 Timothy 5:8
3 Nephi 24:5	Deuteronomy 24:19
Mormon 8:40	Proverbs 15:25

validity of our testing in mortality depends on free agency. Our ability to become like him depends on our free agency. He rarely interferes even when injustice is being done. To do so would jeopardize agency and the plan we chose.

But God can give comfort to those who suffer unjustly. And he does. He can bless those that mourn for whatever reason. And he does. What's more, he is forever teaching right. Note how in every dispensation, including our own, the Lord has warned nations that they will be judged by how well they treat widows and orphans.

By orphans, the scriptures usually mean fatherless children. The theme is particularly noticeable in the Book of Mormon where it is repeated more often than in other scriptures. Following the final destruction of his people, Moroni reiterated that theme once again in a poignant warning to modern times. He speaks of the day when his writings shall come forth and the people of that day, whom he says the Lord Jesus Christ has shown him, and he asks those people a direct question: "Why do ye build up your secret abominations to get gain, and cause that widows should mourn?" (Morm. 8:40) Clearly the Lord does not wish nor has he ever wished for women or their children to suffer any unfairness.

Since I'm on the subject, let me mention one particular scripture I've been repeatedly questioned about. It is the passage in Doctrine and Covenants 132:16 which reads: "Therefore, when they are out of the world they neither marry nor are given in marriage; but are appointed angels in heaven, which angels are ministering servants, to minister for those who are worthy of a far more, and an exceeding, and an eternal weight of glory." Stated bluntly, that scripture seems to say that if one does not marry for time and all eternity in this life he or she will end up being a servant to those who did. Not a very palatable prospect.

The next line says, "For these angels did not abide my

law; therefore, they cannot be enlarged, but remain separately and singly, without exaltation." So it seems to me that the question to ask is: how does one abide the law so that he or she can receive exaltation? So that he or she can be among the exalted, not the servants?

The Savior answers that question several verses later when he says: "But if ye receive me in the world, then shall ye know me, and shall receive your exaltation. . . . This is eternal lives—to know the only wise and true God, and Jesus Christ, whom he hath sent. I am he. Receive ye, therefore, my law" (D&C 132:23–24).

The only one any of us needs to accept into our lives in order to achieve exaltation is Jesus Christ. If you know the scriptures you can resist the suggestion that any blessing is predicated on anything other than individual worthiness and righteous desires, including the desire for an eternal mate. Moreover, we can never be deprived eternally because of the unrighteous choices of others. The prophet Isaiah describes the coming Millennium by saying: "Sing, O barren, thou that didst not bear; break forth into singing, and cry aloud, thou that didst not travail with child: for more are the children of the desolate than the children of the married wife, saith the Lord" (Isa. 54:1). He is speaking specifically of children, but I think the broader meaning extends to any blessing we desire and are worthy to receive, but have not yet received for whatever reason.

What can a single sister get from a study of the scriptures? The pat answer is inspiration, an eternal perspective, knowledge of the plan of salvation, the Atonement, and other gospel principles. That's a good answer. The same is true of anyone who seeks enlightenment from the sacred texts. But it is also true that we bring to such a study our own needs and questions, the pursuit of which allows us to find our own particular light.

"I have no husband," the woman in Samaria confessed

to Jesus as they both stood by Jacob's well.

He answered, "Thou hast well said, I have no husband: For thou hast had five husbands; and he whom thou now hast is not thy husband."

With her whole life laid before her, what could she say? She acknowledged Christ's prophetic powers and then she asked the question troubling her. The Samaritans worshipped one way and the Jews another. She wanted to know which was right.

Jesus answered her such that she began to wonder who he was. She said, "I know that Messias cometh."

Jesus said to her, "I . . . am he."

And in that way, the woman at the well came to know her Savior. What did she do with that knowledge? She told the others in her village and the scriptures say that "many of the Samaritans of that city believed on him for the saying of the woman" (John 4:17-39).

I'm no smarter today than I was when I talked to that Unitarian minister. I still don't understand how eternal companions, sealed families, and many levels of glory will all come together to form an exalted world of absolute joy and absolute fairness for every worthy individual in the life to come. I'm told that it's beyond my comprehension, and I have no trouble believing that. It may not be important for me to understand the details. What I need to know with absolute assurance is that how I feel matters. My feelings will be a determining factor. If that were not so, how could it be heaven?

The Book of Mormon describes our entrance into heaven saying, "the keeper of the gate is the Holy One of Israel; and he employeth no servant there . . . for he cannot be deceived" (2 Ne. 9:41). Deceived? Deceived as to what? As to our truest and deepest feelings. Only Jesus Christ can fully understand, and that is why he alone stands at the gate, ensuring that no mistake can be made. That is how much it matters.

What does not matter is whether a woman is single or married, rich or poor, young or old, brilliant or beautiful. Every woman and every man faces the same challenge—to find that gate where the Savior waits. And how do we find the gate? By seeking to know our Savior so that we will recognize him. By nurturing ourselves, by letting go of our unfounded fears, discovering who we are, loving ourselves, not judging.

If finding a true and loving companion is one of your challenges, know that no one escapes trials and disappointments in this life. Our trials and disappointments just come in different varieties. Know also that you can count on the Savior's love. He never abandons or disappoints. He is ever tender towards our feelings, and single or not, we would all do well to regularly remind each other of that. We all need that kind of assurance.

And note the examples from scripture of our single sisters. Take heart from the courage and contributions of those women. Then go forth and make your own contribution, knowing that all things will work towards your good. How could it be otherwise?

Note

1 Information on Vienna Jaques was drawn from Church Archive sources and other historical records; also *Women's Exponent* 7 (1 July 1878): 20; 8 (15 June 1879): 12; 8 (1 July 1879): 20–21; 9 (15 June 1880): 13; 9 (1 January 1881): 116; 12 (1 March 1884): 152; "Extracts from H. C. Kimball's Journal," *Times and Seasons* 6 (15 March 1845): 838–40; Joseph Smith, *History of the Church* 1:342, 368, 407–8; and Saints Herald, 15 October 1935, p. 1329. See also Elder's Licenses 1836–46, p. 14; PB 41:251; 5:113; Nauvoo Temple Endowment Register 179, 285; Journal History of the Church 21 June 1847, p. 50; Salt Lake City Cemetary Book A, 1848–90. Copy of Daniel Sherer Will dated 20 July 1843, Salt Lake City, provided by Sherwin Chase of Santa, Barbara California.

Where Are the Young Women in Scripture?

On the night of September 21, 1823, a young man who described himself as "being of very tender years" knelt in his bedroom and asked forgiveness. He was not guilty of any great sins, he explained, but he had made foolish mistakes, some of them because he was young, and sometimes "displayed the weakness of youth."

As he prayed, a heavenly messenger appeared. After telling this young Joseph Smith of a sacred book, breastplate, and "seers" (the Urim and Thummim) that were hidden in a hill nearby, the angel went on to quote several prophecies that he said would soon be fulfilled. During that night and on into the next morning the angel Moroni repeated those prophecies four times, impressing deeper and deeper on this young man the importance of the events about to unfold and his role . . .

That was a story that never failed to inspire my seminary students, many of whom were no older than Joseph Smith when he received his first important visions. They seemed to have no trouble identifying themselves as being among the generations saved for the last days to prepare the way for the Second Coming of Christ.

The year that we studied the Book of Mormon, they were similarly impressed with Nephi who described himself as "exceedingly young" (1 Ne. 2:16) and then stepped forward to declare, "I will go and do the things which the Lord hath commanded" (1 Ne. 3:7).

And the year we studied Old Testament, we got quite involved with David and his "thirty"—young men so skilled at war they could hurl a stone or shoot an arrow with either their right or left hand (1 Chron. 12). David was proud of the loyalty and skills of his young men. He praised them in public and wrote psalms about their victories, but it wasn't on skills and loyalty alone that he relied. When David and his thirty escaped King Saul's court to take up the fight against what had become a corrupt government, they fled not to an army base, but to Ramah (1 Sam. 19:18–20), where Samuel was holding a "school of the prophets."

Engaging stories all . . . and yet no matter how engaging the stories, how universal the application of the lessons, sooner or later the inevitable question would arise: Where are the young women in scripture?

66

I assured my young women students that the spiritual qualities that Joseph Smith, Nephi, and David exhibited were the same ones women needed to build their own lives. They knew that. They wanted something else—the assurance that the efforts and faithfulness of young women were noticed. And mattered—then as well as now. Without role models, without stories, that's a hard point to get across.

Young women growing up in the Church today have studied the scriptures from Primary. They know the sacred texts as has no previous generation. What's more, they are of the valiant spirits held back to come forth in this dispensation. They hunger for righteousness. As teachers and leaders our challenge is not to quell their questions, but to feed them material worthy of their concerns.

With that in mind, I offer the following catalogue. Admittedly many of these stories are too brief to make them the focus of a lesson. But they do provide enough to stimulate interest and discussion. I'm more concerned that even stories of young women that are well developed in scripture are not often used in lessons or too often used with misplaced emphasis. Take the story of Esther for example:

ESTHER was a young woman when her uncle Mordecai took her to the king's palace and offered her as a contestant vying to become the queen. But too often her participation in that beauty pageant is emphasized to the overshadowing of deeper qualities. Esther rejected the accouterments of outward appearance. When it came time for her to appear before the great Ahasuerus, she chose not to adorn herself with fine clothes, jewels, or perfumes. Seemingly she realized that she would need more than mere beauty to distinguish herself. Note also that when she agreed to risk her life to save her people, she made only one request: "Go gather all the Jews that are present in Shushan and fast for me, and neither eat nor drink three days, night or day: I also and my maids will fast likewise" (Esth. 4:16). What does that reveal about Esther?

67

While Esther saved her people, the DAUGHTER OF JARED destroyed her nation (see Ether 8:8–17; 9:4–7). First she urged her father to avail himself of Satan's secret combinations; then she plotted with him to overthrow the king, her grandfather. From that time forward the Jaredite nation struggled against the practices of those who engaged in secret combinations—which finally were that nation's downfall. Can a young "capable" woman's actions have far-reaching consequences?

HAGAR was a young slave when Sarah proposed that she be joined with Abraham (see Gen. 16:1–16; 17:20; 21:8–21; 25:12; Gal. 4:24–25). Her haughtiness at being able to produce the one thing her mistress most desired—a child—is understandable. But she was humbled when Sarah wouldn't allow such aires and again when the Lord sent an angel commanding her to return and submit to her mistress. Does that seem fair? And yet the Lord continued to send angels to instruct and provide for Hagar—angels that promised her and her son great blessings. Sarah apparently received no such angelic visitations—at least none were recorded in the sacred writings. The Lord loves us all alike, but he gives us different blessings. Why?

An example that can be difficult but allows for discussion is the DAUGHTERS OF ONITAH (Abr. 1:8, 11–12). Their steadfastness can be admired. They allowed themselves to be killed rather than bow down to idols. However, if one reads on, one realizes that as soon as Abraham was placed on that same altar, it was split in half by God, and the Pharaoh's priests were killed that Abraham might be saved. If God intended such a display of wrath, why did he not do it in time to save the daughters of Onitah as well?

Or, remembering the story of Shadrach, Meshach, and Abed-nego who were protected by angels when they were thrown into the fiery furnace of King Nebuchadnezzar for the same reason—a refusal to worship idols—one has to ask: Where were the angels that might have protected the three daughters of Onitah?

No one knows why God saved Abraham and Shadrach, Meshach, and Abednego. Some say it was necessary that they live to fulfill his purposes. But the scriptures record many instances where faithful servants of both sexes were not spared from the wrong use of free agency by others. Did God care less about what happens to them? Did fewer angels guard them? Of course not. But how do we know that?

These are clearly not easy questions to answer, but I know from experience that my young women seminary students appreciate having the deeper issues of life acknowledged—even when there are not immediate answers. In the face of such dilemmas, the necessity for faith becomes real.

Another challenging story is that of JEPHTHAH'S

DAUGHTER (Judg. 11:31–40). Her father, Jephthah, bargained with the Lord. If God would deliver him "without fail" from the Ammonites, Jephthah promised to "offer . . . up for a burnt offering . . . whatsoever cometh forth of the doors of my house to meet me" (Judg. 11:31). The Lord then delivered Jephthah and his army from the Ammonites, and what came out to meet him was his daughter, his only child. Jephthah was distraught. He "rent his clothes" in anguish. He then explained his promise to his daughter.

It needs to be noted that nowhere in the story does the Lord request that Jephthah sacrifice his daughter, as the Lord requested that Abraham offer Isaac. Jephthah's vow was his own idea. What's more, such human sacrifice was strictly forbidden (see Lev. 18:21; 20:2–5; Deut. 12:31; 18:10), and further the law had provided the means of redeeming a sacrifice (see Lev. 27:1–8). Her father had only to make such an offering in her stead. Others clearly felt that Jephthah's zeal was misguided.[1] Yet Jephthah's daughter accepted her fate, asking only two months to "bewail my virginity"—meaning that she wanted to mourn with her friends the fact that she would not live a full life knowing children and grandchildren. Then the scriptures say that she "returned unto her father, who did with her according to his vow."

The account goes on to say that it became the custom "to lament the daughter of Jephthah" every year. I'm moved to wonder what was mourned—her loss, or her foolishness in submitting to something that clearly was not "of God." Sacrifice means "to make sacred," and this story does not make Jephthah's daughter sacred. She dies to please her father, accepting his idea of what she should do with her life.

The story brings up difficult questions but could offer an opportunity to discuss whose decisions a young woman should accept to govern her life. If a father says that she should be sacrificed, should she accept that as law? How does a daughter determine when she's being ruled in righteousness? How much responsibility must she take for her own life? And what about the rashness of her father's act?

By contrast, one of the fullest and most positive stories of a young woman concerns NAAMAN'S WIFE'S MAID (see 2 Kgs. 5:2, 4). This young woman was captured in a war and carried off to Damascus as a slave of the Syrian field commander Naaman. She had every reason to feel unfortunate and ill-treated. But when she saw that her master suffered from leprosy, the young woman suggested to her mistress that she knew a way for him to be cured. A man of God named Eliseus lived in Samaria, she said and added, "he would certainly have healed him of the leprosy which he hath." Something about this young girl inspired the mistress and then the master to believe that she knew what she was talking about. Naaman went to his king and made arrangements to visit the prophet—all on the word of his wife's servant. And when he saw the prophet, he was cured. How does one inspire such confidence in another?

Jesus raised JAIRUS' DAUGHTER from the dead (see Matt. 9:18–25; Mark 5:35–43; Luke 8:41–56). She was the only child of the ruler of the synagogue. Her father beseeched Jesus to heal her, but before Jesus could make his way to the house, the message came: "Thy daughter is dead." Jesus responded, "Be not afraid, only believe" (Mark 5:36). Then he came to where the young woman lay and raised her. The scriptures say that following that incident, "the fame hereof went abroad into all that land" (Matt. 9:26). That fame must have brought many to the young woman's door wanting to know the truth of what had happened. How did she testify of him who had raised her?

At a time when women had no property rights and

couldn't even inherit land when their father left no son, the FIVE DAUGHTERS OF ZELOPHEHAD—Mahlah, Noah, Hoglah, Milcah, and Tirzah—asked Moses to give them their father's inheritance, an unheard of notion (see Num. 26:33; 27:1; 36:11; Josh. 17:3). Moses took their request to the Lord and was told, "The daughters of Zelophehad speak right." So Moses wrote a new law: "If a man die, and have no son, then ye shall cause his inheritance to pass unto his daughter" (Num. 27:8). When is it appropriate to question laws, customs, or authority? Did the actions of the daughters of Zelophehad require courage? Do you imagine that others in their time might have considered them uppity and disrespectful? What did the Lord say about them?

MARY THE MOTHER OF THE SAVIOR (see Matt. 1:16–23; 2:11; 13:55; Mark 3:31–35; 6:3; Luke 1:27–56; 2:16–48; John 19:26–27; Acts 1:14; Mosiah 3:8; Alma 7:10; 19:13) was a teen when the angel appeared to her, announcing that she would be the mother of Jesus and be known far and wide as "blessed among women." But at first the message confused her. She was a virgin, and so with clear certainty as to that fact, she questioned how the birth could be. Only when it was explained did she submit, saying, "Behold the handmaid of the Lord." But she was agreeing to more than just becoming the mother of Jesus. She was taking on an eternal commitment. Did she understand that? What must she have taken on faith, and what was sure knowledge?

One of the DAUGHTERS OF ISHMAEL must have been an eloquent speaker (see 1 Ne. 7:19). She stepped between Nephi and his older brothers when they intended to kill or injure him and argued so persuasively that they fell at their younger brother's feet and asked his forgiveness instead. What could this young woman have said that would so change Laman and Lemuel's hearts? NEPHI'S WIFE tried to aid Nephi in a similar fashion on board the ship (1 Ne. 18:19).

We only know one thing about NEPHI'S SISTERS (see 2 Ne. 5:6)—that they followed him. But how did his sisters know to follow Nephi instead of Laman? By tradition Laman should have become the head of the family following the death of their father. What did these young women know that caused them to choose right?

And while we are discussing the Book of Mormon, do you remember THE YOUNG WOMEN OF LEHI-NEPHI who saved their families from a Lamanite army? (See Mosiah 19:13–14.) Their courage might be noted in lessons. And what about the SISTERS OF THE YOUNG STRIPLING WARRIORS so admired by Helaman in the Book of Mormon? (Alma 53; 56:47–48) Do you think that the mothers who succeeded in instilling such great faith in their sons gave less to their daughters?

THE TWENTY-FOUR KIDNAPPED DAUGHTERS OF THE LAMANITES (see Mosiah 20; 21:20; 23:30–34; see also Mosiah 25:12; Alma 25:4–9; 43:13) must have expected that their lives would be different. They had every reason to hate the men who captured them and forced them to become their wives. Yet they later saved their wicked husbands' lives. Are these actions inconsistent? What do you do if your life doesn't turn out the way you think it should?

In the New Testament in the book of Acts, we find a YOUNG WOMAN WITH A SPIRIT OF DIVINATION (see Acts 16:16–23) who had been earning her masters a great deal of money with her soothsaying. That is, until she began following the Apostle Paul, saying, "These men are the servants of the most high God, which show unto us the way of salvation." She did this for many days until Paul, being grieved, ordered the spirit to leave her. That caused her masters to be upset at the loss of their income, and they had Paul thrown into prison. How did this young woman know Paul represented the most high God? Can you know a truth by the wrong source? And what happened to her after she was freed of the spirit? Was she also freed of the evil masters who were using her for their gain?

In a similar incident, a mother came to Jesus asking him to cleanse her DAUGHTER OF AN UNCLEAN SPIRIT (see Mark 7:25–30) and was rebuffed. But the mother did not give up. She asked again, saying that surely the Savior would not begrudge her daughter a crumb of consideration. He was impressed with that plea and healed the young girl. How badly did this mother want her daughter's life to be better? How did she know to go to the Savior for this miracle? What do young women today owe to the courage and tenacity of their mothers?

PHILIP'S DAUGHTERS were four unmarried sisters who prophesied (see Acts 21:9). Their father was among the seven set aside to administer the business of the Church. A Greek-speaking Jew of liberal sympathies, he played an important part in spreading the gospel to the Gentiles. He finally settled in Caesarea, where he came to be known as the father of these spiritually gifted young women. More often a young woman is known by her father—taking his name, his residence. Leviticus 21:9 says that a daughter who "profanes" herself through unchastity also profanes her father if he is a priest. Can a daughter's spirituality aid her father? And what about young women prophesying? One of the scriptures that the angel Moroni repeated to Joseph Smith was Joel 2:28 which looks forward to a time when sons and daughters will prophesy. What does that mean? How does one develop the spiritual gift of prophesy?

SHALLUM'S DAUGHTERS (see Neh. 3:12) offer a fine and fairly full example, but their story is little known. When the prophet Nehemiah returned to Jerusalem to rebuild that city's walls, Shallum's daughters were among his supporters. Although their father was wealthy and powerful, a ruler over half the city, these young women were not too proud to join in the menial labor—carrying stones, mud, and mortar when that was what was needed. Faced with opposing political groups who threatened to stop the work, those who understood Nehemiah's vision worked with one hand holding their weapons and one hand holding their tools.

BARZILLAI'S DAUGHTER (see Ezra 2:61–63; Neh. 7:63–65; D&C 85:12) is an example of how a repeated brief reference might be used to open an important discussion. When this young woman married, she kept her father's name, probably because she inherited a hugh estate and wanted the land to be known by her family name. However, her descendants, whose genealogy could not be proved, were denied the priesthood "until there stood up a priest with urim and with thummim," meaning a priest able to discern worthiness even without such records. This incident is again referred to in the Doctrine and Covenants as being true of all apostates. The problem was not that Barzillai's daughter kept her father's name, but that families had become careless in guarding their spiritual heritages. What spiritual heritages do we need to guard?

In a messianic psalm (see Ps. 45) David sings of a time

when a KING'S DAUGHTERS will greet the Savior, bring him gifts, and stand on his right side. "With gladness and rejoicing . . . they shall enter into the king's palace." All young women are daughters of the most high king—king's daughters. What gifts shall they bring him when they enter into his palace?

THE WISE AND FOOLISH VIRGINS (see Matt. 25:1–3). In one of his most beautiful parables, Jesus told of his Second Coming by singling out ten young women as representative of those who would be awaiting him and that great event. Five had sufficient oil in their lamps. Five did not and were disappointed, being refused admittance into the marriage feast. What does the oil represent? How can we be sure we have sufficient? What does the marriage feast represent? Why would not only young women but everyone be disappointed to be refused admittance? Notice also that feminine symbols cluster around scriptures pertaining to the Second Coming, the millennial reign, and Zion as the City of God. Many in the early Mormon church believed these scriptures to be saying that women will have a role in bringing all that to pass. What's more, the scriptures say that unlike any dispensation before it, babes and sucklings in this dispensation will have the word of God (see D&C 128:18). That is what is most exciting about the scriptures. They are not old. Today's newspaper is old: it reports only things that have happened. The scriptures are full of exciting prophecies and visions of what is to come. The scriptures are ever new.

JOSEPH SMITH'S SISTERS, KATHERINE AND SOPHRONIA, saved the gold plates from some men who hoped to steal and sell them. These young women held, carried, and even slept with the plates to protect them, although they never were given the privilege of seeing them without a covering over them. Were they sure of the plates' existence? How sure were they that their brother was engaged in an important work? How did they feel about being persecuted because of him? Did they ever say he wasn't a prophet?

There are other stories and other references to young women in scripture—Job's daughters, Lot's daughters, Rhoda . . . And there are certainly other interpretations of the ones I've offered here. But hopefully I've given a sense of what I see as the potential in these examples.

My great-great grandmother wrote a will at a time when few women in England wrote wills. It's an interesting and somewhat poignant document. She kept a shop in which she had worked all her life, but at the time, according to English law, a woman could not own property and therefore had no need to write a will unless she earned goods after her husband's death—goods that would not have been covered by his will. This was her case. Her husband had died in a fall off a roof, and after his death through her continued work she had amassed a few things that she could legally call her own. She notes these circumstances in her will and claims her right to dispose of her "earned" things. She lists them: several geese, a desk, some linen, a pair of candlesticks, a platter . . . She leaves them to her only daughter, specifying that if her daughter married, these items were not to be considered "dowry" and therefore passed over to her husband. She wanted her daughter to have some things she could call her own.

My great-great grandmother had been married to a good man. She had no reason to think her daughter wouldn't also marry a good man who would love and protect and care for her. Writing her will was not the act of a malcontent. She simply wanted her daughter to have the pride and sense of self that comes with the responsibility of ownership.

Similarly the young women in my seminary classes expressed no rebelliousness in their question: "Where are the young women in scripture?" They simply wanted something to call their own—stories about young women like themselves. Stories in which they could take pride and draw self-assurance. The stories are there. As leaders and parents, we need only pass them on as part of our daughters' inheritances. And let our sons be edified by the examples as well.

Note

[1] Josephus, *Antiquties of the Jews*, chapter VII, vv. 9–12 and footnote.

What We Can Learn from the Unrighteous Women in Scripture

I saved the life of a baby deer the other day.

I lived three blocks from Cadwalder Park, which is not as well known but is similar to Central Park in New York City, both having been designed by the same landscape architect. I mention that because if you've seen one, you can imagine the other. On one end of Cadwalder is a pen with thirty to forty deer that the neighborhood children feed stale bread, poking the pieces through the high wire fence and giggling when soft animal mouths tickle their palms. That's about as bucolic as things get in Trenton, New Jersey.

I was walking along the side of the park when my dog suddenly started sniffing and pulling at her leash. She'd spotted a fawn outside the deer pen, its mother mewing to it through the fence. My dog is a basset hound, smallish and normally quite docile. I realized that if she was eager to chase this little deer, the next bigger dog that came along would probably kill it.

I looked around, and saw no one else. So I figured it was up to me: I had to save this little fawn.

I tied my dog to a post and wading into mud deeper than the tops of my Reeboks, I cornered the fawn against the side of an earthen bank where the brook trickles out of the park. Then I grabbed him. I'm sure I would have been proud of the fact that I managed to catch him on my first try, if I'd had time to think about it. But I had about thirty-five pounds of deer in my arms, and he wasn't Bambi.

He kicked with sharp little hooves and let out a high-pitched wail that brought all the other deer to my side of the park and set my dog off. Basset hounds don't bark—they bay. Mine started up a chorus that should have awakened the dead, but it didn't bring anyone to my aid.

Meanwhile in its struggle, the deer knocked its head against my chin and bloodied its own nose. It was now bleeding all over the front of me. Not bad enough. It had also managed to catch one hoof in my pants pocket, ripping it irreparably; then it urinated all down my side.

Still I managed to hang onto him as I climbed back up the bank to the roadway. I sat with him a few minutes and got him calmed. Then carrying him under my arm, I worked my way around the fence. I hoped to find where he'd gotten out, poke him back inside, and then call the city parks department and tell them to come and fix the fence.

But the deer enclosure is at least half a mile long and probably a quarter mile wide. Halfway around, when I still hadn't found the hole, two things nagged at me: my arms were aching, and I remembered reading somewhere that Lyme Disease comes from deer ticks. So I crossed the street, bruised, bloodied, muddied, with a deer under my arm, and started ringing doorbells. Nine houses later I got someone to call the city and request that a parks person come and open the gate for me. Naturally the employee in charge of the deer pen was out and couldn't be reached. So I sat on the curb of the street and tended the fawn for an hour and a half until the animal keeper finally showed up.

Don't get me wrong. I'm glad I saved that deer's life. But I'd be lying if I suggested that the actual experience was something I'd like to repeat. Why? And what does saving a fawn have to do with the lessons we can learn from the unrighteous women in scripture?

I think the answer to both questions is discernment.

Saving the fawn was difficult because the little animal had no way to determine my intentions. It had no powers of discernment. Instinctively it assumed I meant it harm and reacted accordingly. On the other hand, my own expectations were almost as naive. I saw a baby deer, equated its cuteness with the cartoon character Bambi, and expected only warm, loving appreciation for my good deed. Saving a deer's life is not supposed to ruin half a morning, a pair of Reeboks, and my best jogging pants.

Or is it? Is there any reason why I should think that doing good is free and brings only rewards while doing evil has a price and always brings bad consequences? I mean, if it were that simple, I think I would worry a lot less about how to teach my kids what is truly valuable in life. I think we would need fewer jails, maybe fewer divorce courts. Surely there would be less anguish because few of us set out to seek pain and disappointment. Oh, if it were only that simple! But from such simplicity, we would learn little.

80

What I think we can learn from the unrighteous women found in scripture is how to be a bit more discerning when it comes to good and evil, and we need that sophistication today more than in any previous age. For while the message of evil hasn't changed, the variety of ways by which that message can be delivered has increased.

Lately I have been reading the journals of pioneer women. One theme I've encountered over and over is how these women ached for music and entertainment—something to enliven the daily routine of their lives. I can't help contrasting that with my own circumstances. I rent movies often, sometimes three at a time. The stereo in my house plays almost constantly, and when I get in my car, I turn it on there, too. The day I was out walking and noticed the little deer, I had my Walkman on and was listening to an opera. That adds richness to my life. We all know these same means of communication can also be used to subvert basic values, yet separating the enriching from the potentially degrading is not a simple, straightforward task. Evil doesn't step on stage in a black cape, tall hat, and long mustache as if in some melodrama and say, "Here I am. I'm the villain," any more than good appears always fair-haired and a little too bland to be exciting.

Most of the Christian world believes that if our mother Eve had been able to control herself, we would be living in paradise still. But scriptures restored and revealed in this dispensation will not allow us to believe that Eve disrupted God's plan. Instead we know that she embraced it, making it possible for us, her children, to be born into conditions that allow us to experience both good and evil and, unlike the little deer, learn to distinguish between the two. Eve considered embracing mortality a valuable step forward. In the fifth chapter of Moses she is described as being "glad" and saying, "Were it not for our transgression we should never have had seed and never should have known good and evil" (v. 11).

But while modern scripture corrects our notions about Eve, these same texts provide other examples of women choosing wickedness with chilling consequences. Noah's granddaughters, for example, are singled out as one cause of the great flood (see Moses 8:14-15).

But let's start with the most famous of these women— Jezebel (1 Kgs. 15–22; 2 Kgs. 9–10). Her name is even found in some dictionaries with the meaning of a "shameless or painted women"; in other words, a woman who wears too much makeup and clothing that is gaudy or immodest. But if you think it was her makeup or her clothes that made Jezebel evil, you need to think again. Jezebel's problem was far greater than a "shameless immodesty."

Jezebel was a Phoenician princess at a time when the Phoenicians were an immensely wealthy and influential nation. They believed their wealth and success was due to blessings from their goddess Ashtoreth and her husband, the god Baal. For that reason, they championed the worship of their deities wherever their trade and influence reached throughout the Mediterranean and Middle East.

By contrast, Israel at that time was considered a poor, upstart nation that worshipped a strange, single, invisible god. When Jezebel was married to King Ahab of Israel, as part of a political alliance, she had to have been disappointed. It was not a match worthy of a Phoenician princess. Obviously she decided to assuage her disappointment with action. She would change things.

According to the scriptures, she arrived in Israel with four hundred "prophets" of Ashtoreth and four hundred and fifty "prophets" of Baal, fully intending to supplant Israel's religion with that of her own—a religion that included the worship of trees as symbols of fertility and sexual rites that were more like orgies, giving rise to the oft-used phrase in scripture, "whoring after foreign gods."

One of Jezebel's first acts was to order the extermination of the "prophets" of Jehovah. These are described as priests who were attached to various villages and who performed priestly functions. How many of these prophets were killed by Jezebel is not known. But the scriptures say that one hundred were saved by Obadiah, the governor of the royal household, including the prophet Elijah, who would become Jezebel's chief opponent. Theirs would become a twenty-seven-year-long struggle in which Jezebel would prove herself a formidable opponent, even for a prophet as great as Elijah.

One day in the midst of this religious persecution, Elijah appeared before King Ahab and predicted three years of drought to be followed by a great famine. Elijah knew that the idols of Baal and Ashtoreth were thought to control the weather. So by sealing the heavens, he struck a blow directly at the heart of Jezebel's religion. Her priests could pray all they wanted, but there would be no rain. Then, having made his prophecy, Elijah disappeared.

How do we meet evil and answer it? Elijah did not concern himself with how Jezebel dressed or how she made up her face or even that she was from a foreign country with different customs. She was promoting the worship of fertility gods, so Elijah sealed the heavens and dried up the fertility of the whole countryside. What better or more direct answer could he have given?

At the same time he didn't let King Ahab off. Ahab had been a distinguished soldier, but as a ruler he was weak, and some had thus excused his wickedness by blaming it on his foreign wife. But Elijah knew that Ahab had been an idolater before he married Jezebel. He let the king know that having a foreign wife was no excuse. You can't blame someone else for your sins.

King Ahab and Jezebel hunted for Elijah for three years and couldn't find him, nor did the drought that gripped the whole land break. Obviously, Elijah didn't seem to think it was necessary to continually contend with the king and queen. Having met Jezebel's evil squarely, he didn't stand around and haggle. When he did return, it was with another challenge: his God against Baal to see which one of them could be enticed to rain fire out of heaven to light an offering on an altar.

The priests of Baal had likely performed their ritual, with its attendant magic, many times or they would not have accepted Elijah's challenge. But this time something went wrong. They tried and tried to no avail. Elijah taunted them and their impotent god. When it was his turn, he poured water over the offering and then drew fire from heaven in a triumphant vindication of Jehovah.

But Jezebel was not impressed. She swore revenge, forcing Elijah into hiding, fearful for his life. It was while she was still hunting for Elijah, that she decided to teach her husband a lesson on how to be a "real king."

It seems that her husband wanted a certain vineyard and offered to buy it from the owner, a man named Naboth. But Naboth refused to sell, saying that the vineyard had been in his family for many years and he wished to give it to his own children. King Ahab felt badly but accepted that answer.

Jezebel was outraged. Where she came from, kings could have anything they wanted. No one refused a royal request and lived. She intended that her husband would be such a king. So she called an assembly and falsely charged Naboth with blaspheming against God. She had him arrested, tried, and condemned by false witnesses she had secured herself. After Naboth was stoned, she seized his property.

84

This high-handed murder of an innocent man brought Elijah out of hiding. He confronted King Ahab one day as the king strolled through his newly acquired vineyard. The prophet was blunt. He told King Ahab that because of this act of wickedness, dogs would lick his blood in the field that he had acquired from Naboth, every male child of his family would be cut off, and Jezebel would be eaten by dogs near the ramparts of the palace.

The king immediately tore his clothes and donned sack-cloth—signs of repentance. Nevertheless, three years after its pronouncement, Elijah's prophecy was fulfilled. In a battle King Ahab was killed and dogs licked up his blood. Jezebel survived, unrepentant, for ten more years. Then when Jehu overthrew the government, she knew her death was certain. She put on her makeup, her jewels, and her finest clothes as a way of proudly flaunting before this upstart general the fact that she was a queen, born to her high station.

Jehu rode into the city, and seeing Jezebel strut on her balcony, he ordered her eunuchs to throw her down, and a team of horses ran over her, killing her. Later, remembering that she was the daughter of a powerful Phoenician king, he gave orders to have her buried. But when his servants went out to find her body, they found only her skull, her feet, and the palms of her hands. The dogs had eaten everything else, as Elijah had predicted.

Unfortunately that was not the end of Jezebel's evil influence. Her daughter, Athaliah, carried her wickedness to Judah, the southern kingdom of Israel (2 Kgs. 11). She had been married to King Jehoram, again the marriage being part of a political alliance. Following the example of her mother, she immediately began promoting the worship of Ashtoreth and Baal among the people of the south. Several years later, when her husband died and her son was killed in a battle, she feared that her own power and influence were at an end. So she ordered the massacre of all heirs to the throne, including all her own grandsons, that she might be the only one left to rule and therefore be made queen.

Her orders would have been carried out completely except for the courage of a woman named Jehosheba (2 Kgs. 11:2), who grabbed one of the babies and hid with him in a closet. Later she took the child to the temple, where he was hidden and allowed to grow up among the temple workers there.

While the child was growing, Athaliah ruled six years. During her reign, she pulled down part of the temple and used the materials to build a sanctuary for Baal. Finally the people rebelled and rallied around the young prince, proclaiming him the rightful ruler. Athaliah screamed, "Treason, treason!" But no one came to her aid. Not wanting to defile the house of the Lord with her blood, the high priest of the temple ordered the guards to remove her to a stable near the king's house where she was slain.

Jezebel and her daughter Athaliah represent real evil. Jezebel's intent was nothing less than to destroy the church of God, kill the prophets, and establish another religion. Her daughter's intentions were similar: she wanted to get gain and power. There's nothing new in that. We all know that seeking wealth and power are often motives that will entice people to unrighteousness. But Athaliah's evil goes beyond that. She sought to thwart the fulfillment of prophecy—to prevent the birth of the Savior. As mentioned earlier, it had been prophesied that a Messiah would be born to the house of David. If Athaliah had succeeded in killing all her grandsons, she would have destroyed that lineage and all possibility of that prophecy being fulfilled. But she did not succeed.

Evil is anything or anyone working against God or trying to frustrate the purposes of God. Jezebel and her daughter Athaliah represent evil on that scale. Elijah, the prophet of God, and Jezebel, the promoter of Baal, were locked in a battle of religions. Each was very articulate. Each claimed to be the true representative of the gods he or she espoused. So how did the righteous people of that day know which one of them to follow?

The same way seekers of truth have always known who to follow—by discerning right from wrong, by judging the fruits of those who do good against the destructions of those who do evil. But in order to do that effectively, each individual must carefully guard that power of discernment—taking care not to let it become clouded with personal sin, which is what I think we learn from the example of Joseph and Potiphar's wife (Gen. 39).

You will remember that Joseph, the son of Jacob, was sold as a slave into Egypt. There he served a man named Potiphar who was captain of the guards. It was while he was in the service of Potiphar that Joseph came to be tempted by the master's wife.

Potiphar's wife had no grand scheme by which she hoped to destroy God's church. She just wanted a little pleasure and may not have thought there was anything wrong in that. She came from a culture and a class of people that would have found such pleasures entirely acceptable. We are told in scripture that she tempted Joseph "day by day." In other words, her passion for him was not a sudden flare of lust; it grew slowly, gathering momentum as her insistence increased.

Joseph was a slave, favored as chief among the slaves, but a slave nevertheless. He had reason to feel that life had been unfair to him and might have taken solace in someone's interest, especially if that interest came from a comely woman. Potiphar's wife may have felt justified by the unfairnesses in her life—chief being the fact that she likely had little say in whom she married. Potiphar, as captain of Pharaoh's guard, was a man of great position. He could marry the wife of his choice; she would have had less say in the matter. So why shouldn't she seek to love Joseph, a young man of character that inspired respect?

She knew nothing of the young man's visionary dreams, had no insight into his soul and the fact that he understood that he could not engage in evil and still retain his ability to discern—to continue to receive inspiration—the dreams he had experienced since his early youth. So one day when they were alone, Potiphar's wife, one of the most prominent women in all Egypt, offered herself to her slave. For such a proposition to be refused must have seemed unthinkable. She was humbling herself and extending to him a great honor. But Joseph's answer was prompt and not subtle, revealing a side of him that probably shattered the woman with its honesty. What she viewed as a romance, he termed a "great wickedness."

She seems not to have understood. She persisted, perhaps thinking she had only to overcome some shyness in him. He continued to refuse. The scriptures say this went on daily. Then came the moment when all possible obstacles were removed. The husband was gone, as were the servants. Joseph came into the house on business, and she embraced him, maybe hoping that her flesh touching his would at last overcome his hesitation. Only this time, not even bothering with his usual excuses, Joseph wrenched himself free, leaving his coat behind.

She screamed. She told her story first to the other male servants of the household and then to Potiphar. Joseph, she insisted, had tried to rape her. She had resisted, and he had fled, leaving his garment behind.

The story was believed—and why not? Graciously condescending, Potiphar's wife identified herself with her servants, speaking of the "Hebrew brought in to mock us." To her husband she spoke arrogantly of the "Hebrew servant" who had been presumptuous. Potiphar was a man of the world; he knew the weaknesses of men. Besides the garment served as proof. Potiphar had Joseph thrown into prison.

Nothing more is said of Potiphar's wife. But Joseph, having preserved his righteousness at such a great price, continued to discern right and wrong. It was his ability to understand spiritual things that allowed him to interpret the Pharaoh's dream when no other of his advisors could. Within a few years Joseph rose to be second in power only to Pharaoh.

The other day, I was driving across Pennsylvania listening to a talk show on the car radio. The announcer introduced a woman who had written a book entitled *Having Fun As the Other Woman* in which she touted the advantages of a single woman getting involved with a married man. She claimed that such an affair, if it was handled right, had no complications, no commitments. It was simply a "romantic interlude with no strings attached," she said. When the announcer questioned her about the possible drawbacks, she simply responded that one had be to smart and careful, but otherwise there were no problems.

I was incredulous to think that anyone seriously believed that an illicit affair did no damage to the individuals involved. This woman did not even allow for the emotional wrenching that would be part of beginning and ending such an affair. To deny those emotions, to deny the psychological and spiritual aspects of any relationship seems tantamount to denying the soul and reducing human beings to mere physical machines—something like the car I was driving. It rolls down the highway no matter who is behind the steering wheel as long as the driver is smart enough not to run it into a tree. Most of us know there is more to being human than that.

But of course there have always been those who thought they could have it both ways. Contrast Joseph's response to Potiphar's wife with Samson's to Delilah (Judg. 13–16). The story is well known, so let me fill in only a few details.

Samson, like Joseph, was a special young man. An angel appeared to Samson's mother and asked her not to eat or drink any unclean thing that her child might be known as a Nazarite from the womb. Why? That's what her husband wanted to know. He wasn't sure he believed his wife had seen an angel until the same heavenly messenger appeared and explained that the child would deliver Israel from the Philistines. But if he was to be successful, he needed special powers that came only from the Spirit.

It was this purity—signified by his diet and not cutting his hair—that gave Samson his physical and his spiritual strength, but unlike Joseph who shunned evil, Samson thought he could toy with it—playing with Delilah, teasing her, making a game of his exploits—and still retain his powers.

As an unrighteous woman, Delilah was probably worse than Potiphar's wife. She was paid like a harlot and worked for the enemies of Israel. But she had no power over Samson that he did not give her. Despite her charms and her good looks, she could not coax anything out of him that he was not willing to tell her.

It was Samson who made the mistake. He thought he could have it both ways—his fun and his future all at the same time. For a while he succeeded. He defeated the Philistines single-handedly. He ridiculed them by beating them with the jawbone of an ass and stealing the gates of their city. But when he thought he could tell Delilah the source of his strength and still keep his powers, he was wrong.

Joseph in Egypt knew that. He refused to compromise himself. He is still regarded as a man of great spiritual vision while Samson is only a great disappointment who never completed the mission the angel said he was born to.

Evil hurts the sinner. It limits progress, curtails potential, hinders development, darkens one's light. This happened to King Saul and is illustrated most aptly by his encounter with the Woman of En-Dor (1 Sam. 28). She is sometimes called the Witch of En-Dor and represents evil of an entirely different ilk. She was a necromancer, practicing the art of communicating with the dead as a means of predicting the future.

It should be noted that an estimated half million European women were accused of being witches and executed between the years of 1300 and 1700 A.D.[1] Today, historians believe that most of those women were not engaged in the black arts. Accusing and executing women for being witches was a means of intimidation—discouraging women from seeking education, occupations or lifestyles other than those narrow roles prescribed for the female sex. The practice was also used to shift blame when economic policies failed, famines persisted, or plagues raged. That is an evil of a different sort and needs to be recognized as such. But that doesn't excuse those who do, indeed, practice the black arts. The Bible clearly warns about such practices, and Moses had made witchcraft a capital offense.

King Saul, in the early part of his reign, enforced that law by killing all those who had "familiar spirits." You will remember that Saul was an outstanding young man whom the Lord chose through the prophet Samuel to become the first king of Israel because of his righteousness. But later in his life, he fell victim to sin and was afflicted with a deep depression. Faced with both domestic and foreign wars, and being unable to discern the prophet Samuel's successor, he was at a loss to know where to turn for advice. So he disguised himself and went to consult the Woman of En-Dor. Specifically, he wanted her to arouse the spirit of the dead prophet Samuel so that he could seek advice of him.

The Woman of En-Dor knew that the art she practiced was punishable by death, and so she was wary of Saul for some time, but eventually she acquiesced to his request and the seance began. Although the woman had no ability to see through Saul's disguise, both she and Saul immediately recognized the apparition claiming to be Samuel when a spirit appeared. In fact, she was so distressed, she screamed that she had seen gods coming up out of the earth.

The spirit called Saul by name and condemned him, predicting that he and his sons would die in battle the next day. Hearing that harsh prophecy, the Woman of En-Dor sought to comfort her guest—the king. She helped him to her bed and offered him something to eat and drink. But that did Saul little good. Though he rested and ate, he could not be consoled. For the Woman of En-Dor had no power to comfort him, and the next day the "prophesy" was fulfilled.

In the end, King Saul's wickedness spilled over to hurt not only himself but his nation. This is a common theme in scripture—the idea that evil spreads and can destroy whole nations. How we choose to live our lives, whether for good or evil, matters significantly, not only to ourselves but to those around us. Consider the daughter of Jared (Ether 8).

She is described in the Book of Mormon as a capable woman, "exceedingly expert" and "exceedingly fair," meaning she was intelligent and beautiful. She also loved her father. Seeing him grieve because he had seized the throne and then been deposed, she decided she would help him win the kingdom back. She knew of ancient oaths and covenants connected to the devil by which men and women had obtained kingdoms and great worldly glory in the past (3 Ne. 6:28). These secret combinations had been known among the children of Adam and Eve since the time of Cain, who first entered into such a covenant with Satan, calling himself "Master Mahan" and glorying in his wickedness (Moses 5:29–33).

The daughter of Jared knew about those secret combinations from "the record which [her] fathers brought across the great deep." She must have been a highly privileged woman, not only educated, but with access to books concealed from most. Such privilege might have been used for good, but the daughter of Jared went to her father and suggested they avail themselves of the power of Satan. She had a definite plan in mind. Her father was to send for Akish, the son of Kimnor, who was the king's friend. Supremely confident in herself, the daughter of Jared said, "I will dance for him, and I will please him, that he will desire me." She suggested that the price for her hand in marriage should be the head of the then ruling king—her grandfather.

Although the Lord warned the king to flee and thus saved his life, Akish and Jared did seize the kingdom as they had planned and made Jared king. In turn, Jared gave his daughter to Akish to be his wife. But that was not the end of it. Akish soon decided that he wanted to be king himself and murdered Jared, the father that the daughter of Jared had loved so much she was willing to engage the forces of hell to help him. But even that was not the end of it. Akish became jealous of his own son and had him imprisoned and starved to death. The other sons of Akish warred against their father until the whole nation was nearly destroyed (Ether 9).

After she married Akish, the daughter of Jared is never mentioned again. One wonders how she felt seeing her father killed, her young son starved in prison. But the scriptures leave no question as to the consequences her actions had upon her nation. Of the kings who followed Akish, some were righteous and some were not, but every one of them had to deal with the secret combinations that the daughter of Jared had unleashed. Eventually it was those secret combinations that destroyed the entire Jaredite nation—all because a capable young woman made a personal decision to enter the devil's league. Hers certainly was a decision that mattered.

Jesus told a parable of the last days in which he described a farmer going out and planting wheat in his field (Matt. 13:24–30). That night, while he slept, an enemy came and sowed tares among his wheat. What could the farmer do? If he pulled up the tares, he would uproot the wheat. So he let them grow together side by side until the harvest time.

We are living in the time described by that parable. It is not always easy to tell the wheat from the tares—the good from the evil. As the examples show, the qualities of courage, loyalty, endurance, and even love can be possessed by both good and evil women. It is not the qualities, but how they are used that makes the difference. Similarly, dancing is not evil because the daughter of Jared used it to plot the downfall of a king; neither is wearing makeup sinful because Jezebel painted her face. Evil is not evil by association but by intent, and sometimes it is hard to know the intent. Like wheat and tares growing together, sometimes we have to wait to see the budding of the fruit as harvest time approaches.

It has always been difficult to identify and combat evil. Elijah certainly didn't find Jezebel an easy opponent. That's why we need to guard our ability to discern. Otherwise we are lost—no better able to guide our lives than that little deer I saved when it couldn't even understand the danger it was in. If there is one thing we should learn from the unrighteous women in scripture, it is to never do anything that will lessen our ability to discern. We can't afford to trade any of that away for any amount of worldly wealth or fame. The challenges we face from evil are too real for that.

On the other hand, the scriptures are full of stories about women who were successful in building their own lives and testimonies, women who succeeded in being of service to others and in aiding the bringing forth of the kingdom of God. In fact there are several examples that show women recognizing righteousness and embracing it under circumstances that seem so spiritually limiting that one wonders how they knew.

One of these was Belshazzar's mother. She was the wife of Nebuchadnezzar and the mother of Belshazzar, the last king of the Babylonian empire where the young Daniel, of lion's den fame, had been taken to serve in the king's court. We know very little about Belshazzar's mother, except that she lived in great courtly splendor. Historians believe she may have ruled Babylonia during one of her husband's illnesses. She is thought to have built beautiful bridges, wharves, tiled embankments, and lakes as civic improvements.[2] She was regarded as the noblest and most beautiful woman of her time. That part of the history may be flattery, but the scriptures flatter her in another way.

In three verses in the book of Daniel, Belshazzar's mother appears and speaks, giving us a glimpse of a woman of far greater understanding than we would have expected from her circumstances (Dan. 5:10–12). Her son, the king, was crazed with drink and had shouted to his butlers to bring the serving cups taken from the Lord's temple at Jerusalem as part of Babylon's plunder. These sacred vessels were filled with wine and then defiled by the lips of the drunken king and his thousand lords attending this great banquet. At the height of the celebration, an apparition in the shape of the fingers of a man's hand wrote on the walls of the great banquet hall, *Mene, Mene, Tekel, Upharsin.* No one knew how to interpret the words.

Hearing of this strange occurrence, Belshazzar's mother came to the banquet hall and advised her son to call for the prophet Daniel who was then an old man. She told her son that Daniel was a man "in whom is the spirit of the holy gods." Then she added, "And in the days of thy father light and understanding and wisdom, like the wisdom of the gods, was found in him."

I'm sure you know the rest of the story. Daniel came and told the king that he had been weighed and found wanting and that his kingdom was to be given to his enemies. What Daniel spoke came true. But how did Belshazzar's mother know that Daniel would be able to interpret the writing? She had been surrounded by counselors, advisors, and so-called "wise men" all her life. How was she able to recognize the one in whom was "the spirit of the holy gods"?

That is an important question. For we all need to be able to recognize the true messengers of our Father amid the din of other voices. And really there is only one way to know— by the spirit that "lieth not," meaning the Holy Ghost. Fortunately, true seekers are always rewarded. No matter our outward circumstances, our honest inward searchings will yield truth, and just as Belsahzzar's mother knew, we can know.

Think about Pilate's wife. When Jesus was brought before her husband to be tried and perhaps put to death, how was it that Pilate's wife was the one person who had the troubled dreams—the one person who warned her husband not to have anything to do with this man? What prompted the Queen of Sheba to come from the far most parts of the earth to visit Solomon to learn of his wisdom? How did she know where to go and whom to seek?

Others can fail to recognize a miracle. One day, Jesus encountered a man who had been blind from birth (John 9). His disciples asked him, "Who did sin, this man, or his parents, that he was born blind?" Jesus answered that neither had sinned—this thing had happened that the glory of God might be made manifest. Then he healed the man.

The Pharisees didn't want anyone to believe this miracle, so they called in the man's parents and questioned them, suggesting that perhaps their son hadn't been really blind. This mother and father, faced with an obvious miracle that should have made them rejoice and sing the praises of him who had healed their son, were fearful. They were afraid they might be banned from the synagogue where they had worshipped all their lives. So when pressed, this couple referred the Pharisees to their son, saying that he was a grown man. The Pharisees could question him. They did not have the courage to say, yes, our son who was blind has been healed.

Seeing a miracle was not enough to kindle the faith of that mother and father. Like Jezebel, who saw Elijah repeatedly work miracles, they failed to discern the deeper spiritual wonder. Yet others like Belshazzar's mother and Pilate's wife seemingly discerned truth enough to keep their spiritual lamps lit while living in near blackness. Discernment is an individual gift that must be kept pure—unclouded by personal sin—or we become less able to recognize evil in any of its forms. This is the lesson we learn from the unrighteous women in scripture.

We also learn that while life might be complicated and made more difficult by individuals who seek to thwart God and his purposes, their plots never succeed. God explained this to Moses and Joshua, saying: "Be strong and of good courage, fear not, nor be afraid of them; for the Lord thy God, he it is that doth go with thee; he will not fail thee, nor forsake thee (Deut. 31:6).

He whispered the same hope to Joseph Smith when he was in Liberty Jail: "And then, if thou endure it well, God shall exalt thee on high; thou shalt triumph over all thy foes" (D&C 121:8).

These promises apply to everyone—except the unrighteous. They have no promise—none at all.

Notes

[1] Erica Jong, *Witches* (New York: Mew American Library, 1981), p. 38. See also Ronald Holmes, *Witchcraft in History* (Secaucus, New Jersey: The Citadel Press, 1977); and Jeffrey B. Russell, *A History of Witchcraft* (London: Thames and Hudson, 1980).

[2] Scholars note a number of historical difficulties in the book of Daniel. Nevertheless, most agree that the woman called "Belshazzar's mother" was likely Notocris, wife of Nebuchadnezzar, who was known to have exercised great influence in court and accomplished many civic improvements. See Edith Deen, *All the Women of the Bible* (New York: Harper & Brothers, 1955).

97

THE WOMEN IN THE SAVIOR'S LINEAGE

Because of an excellent arts program, my son attended a Catholic high school. The first year, he teased the nuns by telling them that he attended early-morning seminary and was going to be made a priest when he was sixteen. They didn't understand. Even his more lengthy explanations left them shaking their heads bemused.

The next year he was required to take a course in world religions. When he filled out his registration card, he wrote "Mormon" in the religion space. The sister teaching that class looked at his card and knowing him to be something of a class clown, questioned that answer.

"Mormon," she said. "What is this here Mormon stuff? I never heard of anything like that. You put down what you really are." This same sister had been outside New Jersey only three times and in a previous history class had referred to western Pennsylvania as "the West."

My son shrugged. "Look it up in a dictionary. There are really Mormons, and I'm one of them."

He came home that day and announced loudly, "I'm going to study world religions with a woman who has never heard of Mormons."

In truth, it was my son who more often showed his ignorance. He was unfamiliar with such common Catholic terms as *eucharist, lent, rosary, mass, stations of the cross,* and *confession.* One day he slipped and called the priest-principal "Dad," instead of "Father."

"I knew it was supposed to be something like that," he explained.

Yet all-in-all, it was a fine experience. At the end of four years, he was left with a fuller understanding and greater appreciation of the Catholic church and the commitment of its members. And those who came in contact with him had then at least heard of the Mormons.

It is because people coming from different backgrounds are more likely to understand the gospel if it is presented in familiar terms that four different versions of Christ's life are included in the New Testament—Matthew's, Mark's, Luke's, and John's. Mark writes to a "gentile" audience. His writing is fast moving and emphasizes the things the Savior did more than the things he said. He often includes explanations of Jewish customs that non-Jewish readers would need in order to understand the narrative. Luke is more polished, a literary gospel. Luke appeals to both Jews and Gentiles, presenting Jesus as the universal Savior of all humankind. He also includes more stories about women than any other gospel writer. John's account lacks some of the fundamental information found in the other gospels because John was writing to members of the Church in his day who already knew the basics. His purpose was to emphasize the divine nature of Jesus as the Only Begotten Son of God.

Matthew wrote his gospel to the Jews and therefore takes great pains to try to persuade them that Jesus is the promised Messiah. To do so, he cites Old Testament prophecies and speaks repeatedly of Jesus as the Son of David. For him and his purposes, the genealogy of the Savior was fundamentally important. The Jews knew that the Messiah would be born into a certain family line, being a descendant of Abraham and David, and so it should not be surprising that Matthew begins: "The book of the generation of Jesus Christ, the son of David, the son of Abraham." He then goes on to outline Jesus' lineage. But his genealogy is not exhaustive: he does not include every individual to be found in the ancestry of the Savior. His list is representative, with emphasis on the portion of the

Savior's ancestry most likely to show the Jews that he was, indeed, the promised Messiah. Knowing that, it is interesting to note who Matthew included in his family outline and who he left out. Of particular interest are the women he names. They are not the obvious choices.

He does not include Eve, "the mother of all living," or Sarah, Abraham's wife, who wanted so desperately to be a part of fulfilling the great promise given her husband, or Rebekah, who knew before her sons were born that the younger would rule over the older. Nor does he include Leah, who, while not the beloved wife of Jacob, was the mother of Judah through whom the Savior would descend.

So who does he include?

Thamar, who is called Tamar in the Old Testament, Rachab, known as Rahab in the Old Testament, Ruth, and "her that had been the wife of Urias," meaning Bathsheba. And at the end, of course, Mary, the mother of Jesus.

These choices seem all the more curious when we remember that Tamar wanted children so badly she was willing to play the harlot to trick her father-in-law into fathering them; Rahab was a harlot in the city of Jericho; Ruth was a Moabite—a foreign woman with whom the Israelites were not supposed to marry—and in taking Bathsheba, King David committed adultery. Yet I think Matthew knew what he was doing when he made those choices. Let's examine the stories closer.

Tamar's story is found in the thirty-eighth chapter of Genesis and revolves around the strong desire women of her dispensation had to participate in the blessing promised their father Abraham. God had promised Abraham that he would make of him a "great nation" through whom "all families of the earth shall be blessed." Included among his numerous posterity would be the Savior of the world. Women of Tamar's day were as focused and aware of that promise as women in this dispensation are about doing missionary work that they might be part of fulfilling the prophecies concerning the Second Coming.

In keeping with this desire to fulfill the promise given Abraham, part of the law had been structured to safeguard a woman's right to her children. A woman widowed with no children was to be married to her husband's brother that she might have children by him. In fact it was forbidden for any impediment to be allowed to stand in the way of a woman having her children (see Deut. 25:5–6).

Tamar was married to the oldest son of Judah, the father of one of the twelve tribes of Israel—the tribe of Judah. But Tamar's husband died before she had any children, so following the law, Judah married Tamar to his next son. But he also died before Tamar had children. That meant Judah had only one son left, and he was too young to marry, so Judah sent Tamar back to her father's house, saying he would send for her when his son was older. However, secretly Judah feared that Tamar was cursed and so never intended to let her marry his youngest son. Time passed, and Tamar began to suspect that her father-in-law did not plan to marry her to his youngest son. Feeling indignant, she sought a way to force Judah to accept his responsibility.

Her plan was not only daring, it involved great personal risk. It was sheep-shearing season and many guests would be coming from the surrounding country for the festival, so Tamar removed her garments of widowhood, put on a veil to hide her face, and "wrapped" herself—a phrase that means she put on colorful festival robes. Then she went and stood by the side of the road, where harlots plied their trade. When Judah came along, he took her for a harlot and asked, "Let me come in unto thee." She answered, "What wilt thou give me, that thou mayest come in unto me?"

Not recognizing her, Judah promised that in the morning he would send her a young goat from his flock.

Still playing the harlot, she agreed, but wanted a pledge to make sure that he would send the goat.

He asked, "What pledge shall I give thee?"

She asked him for his signet ring, his bracelets, and the staff that he carried. In modern terms that might be equiv-alent to a driver's license, major credit card, and social security number. Tamar had requested items of identifica-tion. The scriptures say that Judah then went in unto her and she conceived by him.

Next morning Judah sent the young goat with a friend who was supposed to give it to the harlot and redeem his personal possessions, but his friend could not find her—no one knew of a harlot working in that area.

Three months later, Judah received word that his daughter-in-law was with child. Angered to think she had dishonored his family, Judah ordered that she be brought before the council of the elders, condemned, and burned. Under the law, he was within his legal right—that was the penalty for being with child outside of wedlock.

When she was brought before the council of elders, Tamar produced the signet ring, bracelets, and staff, saying, "By the man whose these are, am I with child . . . Discern, I pray thee whose are these."

They were Judah's. Anyone could have recognized them as belonging to Judah. Forced to admit that he was the father, Judah declared, "She hath been more righteous than I; because that I gave her not to Shelah, my youngest son," acknowledging that he had been wrong to deny Tamar children.

When her time came, Tamar delivered twins. She and one of her sons, Pharez, became direct progenitors of the Savior.

An interesting woman, though I have yet to hear Tamar used as an example in a Sunday School lesson or Sacrament meeting talk. That's not hard to understand. Her actions and those of her father-in-law raise morality questions. Yet Judah is consistently referred to as a "righteous man" and Tamar was pronounced blameless by the council of elders. What are we to make of that?

Perhaps standing before the council of elders was one step in Judah and Tamar's repentance. More likely, we don't know the whole story. But do we ever know the whole story? It is because we are limited in our understanding that the Savior repeatedly warned against making judgments. "Judge not, and ye shall not be judged: condemn not, and ye shall not be condemned: forgive, and ye shall be forgiven" (Luke 6:37). And again, "Judge not according to the appearance" (John 7:24).

This is something to keep in mind as we move on to the next example.

103

After Tamar, Matthew continues through the Savior's genealogy for several generations before he mentions another woman—Rahab. In some ways the inclusion of Rahab is not surprising because hers had always been a favorite story of the Jews. Even today, next to Abraham, Rahab is considered by the Jewish people as a classic example of true hospitality, and we know that her story was being told and retold among the Jews of Jesus' day because she is mentioned twice in the New Testament. Paul reminds the early Christian Hebrews of her faith and so does James (see Heb. 11:31; James 2:25). Rahab was a woman who recognized the followers of the true God and decisively cast her lot with them.

Her story concerns Joshua and the city of Jericho (Josh. 2, 6). You will remember that as Joshua was leading the Israelites into the promised land of Canaan, they encountered the walled city of Jericho standing in their way. Not knowing exactly how to overcome such a city, Joshua called two men and told them to go down into the plain and spy out the land—"Go view the land," he said, "even Jericho."

So the two men went down into Jericho to a harlot's house and stayed there. The harlot's name was Rahab. There have been some Bible commentaries that have tried to suggest that Rahab was an innkeeper—not a harlot. But the scriptures call her a harlot, in the New Testament she is called a harlot, and everything about her story suggests that she was a harlot, as well as an innkeeper. In the New Testament, Jesus acknowledged that some women of the streets may pass into heaven ahead of many of the self-righteous (see Matt. 21:31). He may even have been thinking of Rahab, his ancestor. For despite whatever circumstances brought her to that profession, when Rahab had a chance to escape, she did.

So Joshua's spies went to Jericho and into Rahab's house, but the King of Jericho became suspicious of these strange men and sent his own messengers to Rahab saying, "Bring forth the men that are come to thee, which are entered into thine house; for they be come to search out all the country."

But Rahab was not willing to turn the spies over. She told the king's messengers that her guests had left at dusk, just before the gates were closed. Meanwhile, Joshua's spies were hidden on the roof of Rahab's house under stalks of flax which were drying there. Later that night before she helped the spies escape over the wall, she talked to them as they lay hidden in the stems of flax. I like to think of this as something like a first missionary discussion. Rahab and her people had heard of the Lord's miracles on behalf of the children of Israel, and as she continued to talk to Israel's spies, she seemed to sense a larger truth. She declares herself, saying, "The Lord your God, he is God in heaven above, and in earth beneath."

Having expressed that belief, she asked the spies to spare her and her relatives in the upcoming battle, and they swore by the God of Israel to do so. As the night grew dark, Rahab helped Joshua's spies slip down a cord from the window of her house to the outside of the town wall. They told her to display a scarlet thread from her window so that the attacking forces would recognize her house and save it from destruction.

When Joshua came against the city of Jericho and Jericho's walls came tumbling down, we are told that he kept the promise of his spies. Rahab and all her family and even her home were spared destruction. According to Matthew she married Salmon, son of Naasson, and her son was Booz [Boaz]. That makes her a direct progenitor of King David and Jesus.

It was Rahab's son Boaz who married Ruth, the next woman Matthew names in his genealogy. Her story is well known. What I want to emphasize is that here again Matthew presents a woman, like Rahab, who was willing to forsake her land and her people and all their traditions for the one true god. The magnitude of faith it took for Ruth to cast aside all that she knew for an unknown life in Israel cannot be appreciated unless you know the attitudes and constraints under which she made her decision. Not an easy decision—although in hindsight it seems like the obvious thing to do.

I am perhaps more attuned to the particular anguish behind this kind of decision because of an often repeated family story. My grandparents on my father's side joined the Church in Germany in the 1920s. Then in 1929, my grandfather decided that he wanted to bring his family to America to be closer to the Church and the temple. My grandmother was not quite so willing. She came from a large and close family. They were active in a growing branch of the Church where they were, and she saw no need to leave her family and friends and go to a country where even the language would be foreign. She had already been displaced once by the First World War, her family having lost everything and been forced out of her childhood home when the country of Poland was created by the Treaty of Versailles. She hated the idea of starting all over again. But my grandfather was adamant in his decision, and so she struck a compromise. She would come to America if they would settle in New York City where she knew a few friends from the old country.

Everything was fine until they arrived in America. Then they were informed by American immigration officials that since they were being sponsored by a family in Idaho, they would have to go to that state for the first few years. She refused and found herself incarcerated on Ellis Island faced with deportation. She stubbornly held her ground for three days before she capitulated. My grandfather promised he would bring her back to New York City as soon as it was legal to do so, a promise he was never able to keep, a promise she must have known he'd never be able to keep.

When Ellis Island opened as a national monument, I took my memories of hearing that story and walked the corridors and stood in the prison cells. I tried to appreciate my grandmother's decision. It seems fortuitous now. By leaving Germany in 1930, my grandmother and her family missed the rise of Naziism, the Second World War, and the Russian occupation of her city. But she didn't know that. From her point of view, it made no sense to take her young family to American in the middle of the Great Depression. But she came, leaving her family and her whole previous life behind her.

Ruth, in the Bible, faced a similar decision. Her story begins a generation before with a famine in Bethlehem that forced her husband's parents, Elimelech and Naomi, to move to Moab. In that foreign land, their sons married Moabite women—Ruth and Orpah. But misfortune continued to plague this family, and in a short time Naomi lost Elimelech her husband, and both of her sons, leaving her a widow and her daughters-in-law widows as well.

Without sons or grandsons to support her, an Israelite woman faced dire circumstances, especially if she was far from other family and kinsmen. So Naomi decided to return to Bethlehem, her home. But what would her daughters-in-law do in Israel? The Israelites had been warned repeatedly by their prophets against marrying foreign women because the beliefs of foreign women had repeatedly influenced the Israelites to worship false gods. There was such a strong feeling against accepting foreign women into the community, it was likely her daughters-in-law would be shunned, and Naomi didn't want that. She loved her daughters-in-law. As Moabites, Naomi thought Ruth and Orpah would probably do better in their own homeland with their own families. Naomi explained all this to her daughters-in-law, and Orpah agreed, returning to her father's house.

107

Ruth refused to be so practical because she saw the greater light, had hope in a greater future. And so she clung to her mother-in-law and said: "Intreat me not to leave thee, or to return from following after thee: for whether thou goest, I will go; and where thou lodgest, I will lodge: thy people shall be my people, and thy God my God" (Ruth 1:16).

I think you know the rest of the story of how Naomi and Ruth returned to Bethlehem and Ruth went out to glean the fields as was the right of the poor. There she attracted the attention of Naomi's kinsman, Boaz, and Naomi helped Ruth indicate to Boaz her willingness to marry him. After they were married, Ruth gave birth to a son whom Naomi, in her old age, nursed as if he were her own. The story's happy ending nearly overshadows the decision Ruth made. When she left Moab, she expected nothing but to be able to be with her mother-in-law whom she loved and to be among the people of Israel who worshipped the true God, but she didn't necessarily expect to be accepted by those people. In

Deuteronomy Chapter 23 verse 3 the Israelites had been instructed not to accept a Moabite into their congregation unto the tenth generation. Knowing all of that, Ruth chose to go anyway saying: "thy people shall be my people, and thy God my god." The fact that things worked out better than she could have ever expected was a blessing she couldn't have foreseen—but she trusted. She made the decision.

The fourth woman that Matthew includes in his genealogy is the wife of Uriah, or Bathsheba (2 Sam 11, 12). At first she would seem to be different—less decisive than Ruth or Rahab or Tamar—until you remember that her son, Solomon, was not the heir apparent to David's throne. Not only was he not the birthright son, he was not even the favorite son of King David. It was Bathsheba who won the throne for him.

As you remember, King David saw Bathsheba bathing on her rooftop one day and desired her. I've seen two film versions of this story and both portrayed Bathsheba as being seductive and deliberately tempting David with her nakedness. But that's not how the Biblical account reads. Quite the opposite, for Bathsheba enjoyed the friendship and good graces of the prophet Nathan throughout all the events that happened to her. In fact, she was the "little ewe" with no choice according to the parable that Nathan told David when he exposed the king's guilt. What's more, she is described as coming from a God-fearing family and as the wife of a God-fearing man.

The scriptures simply say that David saw her and sent his messengers with orders to take her. Similarly in scripture, Sarah, Abraham's wife, was twice taken by a king because of her beauty, and Vashti refused to do a king's bidding at great personal cost (Esth. 1, 2). In those days, one did not refuse a king.

Later, when Bathsheba found herself with child, she informed the king, and he was the one who tried to cover up his adultery by calling her husband back from the Ammonitish war—no doubt hoping he would lay with his wife and assume the child was his. David even sent a feast to Uriah's house to help with the festivities. But Uriah was a righteous man. He believed that going to battle where one might kill or be killed required that a soldier be ritually pure. Following that custom, he refused to visit his wife. David tried again, first getting Uriah drunk, and then sending him to see his wife. Again, Uriah refused because he was a soldier prepared for the battlefield. When those attempts failed, David sent him back to the war and at the same time ordered his commander to place him in the thick of the fighting and then draw back from him, so he would be killed.

On hearing of her husband's death, Bathsheba mourned. But that was only her first sorrow. David brought her to the palace and made her his wife, but the child she carried died shortly after birth, and she mourned again.

Years later when David was on his deathbed, Bathsheba intervened at the Prophet Nathan's request and persuaded David to declare her second child, Solomon, the next king (1 Kgs. 1). When the prophet urged her to use her influence to see that rivals did not prevail, she was successful. Her argument to David in behalf of her own life and the life of Solomon shows wisdom, sophistication, and foresight. With those same qualities she probably extended her influence into her son's reign and may have been the inspiration behind Solomon's desire for his own wisdom.

In any case, we again find a woman who was decisive and who used her influence wisely. But I think we should also note that Matthew calls Bathsheba, "Uriah's wife," even though his whole purpose in writing his genealogy is to prove to the Jews that Jesus was a descendant of King David. That reference is particularly interesting because in the Doctrine and Covenants Bathsheba is also called "Uriah's wife"—not David's. Section 132 explains, that because David sinned in taking Bathsheba, he fell from exaltation and will not inherit his wives in the next world, "for I gave them to another, saith the Lord."

It would seem that Bathsheba won her place in the genealogy of the Savior in spite of the sin involved in her being taken by David. That also suggests that she maintained her righteousness through it all—something that could not have been easy.

The women that Matthew included in the genealogy of the Savior are interesting, decisive women—women willing to risk a great deal to be part of the great promise given to Abraham and his posterity. When the angel Gabriel appeared to Mary and told her that she had been selected to be the mother of the Savior, he also told her that she was "blessed among women," because it was an honor to be a part of the Savior's family. The Catholic sisters at my son's high school knew that. Many of them have taken personal vows in that regard and their reverence for Mary is similarly motivated.

But I want to suggest that we can all be part of the Savior's family.

One day Jesus sat in a house surrounded by his disciples when someone told him that his mother and brothers were outside looking for him. He replied, "Who is my mother? and who are my brethren?" Then he went on to answer his own question saying, "Whosoever shall do the will of my Father which is in heaven, the same is my brother, and sister, and mother" (Matt. 12:48, 50).

Jesus is the Savior of all the world. He looks beyond national origin, past sins, and odd circumstances to embrace all who come to him. The five women included in Matthew's genealogy illustrate that. They show what all must do, regardless of our circumstances, to be part of Jesus' family. It is the same thing Jesus has always asked of his followers—that we do his Father's will. It is exactly that simple, that demanding, and that possible. May we all be included in the Savior's family—kinswomen with Tamar, Rahab, Ruth, Bathsheba, Mary, and all women who have the courage to make righteous choices even in difficult circumstances. That is my prayer.

WHAT DOES IT REALLY MEAN TO BE A "MOTHER IN ISRAEL"?

Recently in Relief Society I listened to a discussion comparing the merits of different ways to fix breakfast. It was agreed that breakfast is an important meal, if not the most important meal of the day; that all family members regardless of age or occupation need the nutrition and ready supply of energy a good breakfast provides; and it seemed to be understood that breakfast was primarily the responsibility of the mother in the household. At that point, the discussion broke down into three groups: those who championed the "nurturing mother" who gets up and fixes her family a hot, well-balanced meal every morning, those who favored the "organized mother" who oversees each family member taking a turn at this chore, and those who defended the "efficient mother" who makes sure milk and juice are in the refrigerator and a whole-grain cereal is in the cupboard and lets her family fix their own.

I left that meeting feeling the way I do after most Mother's Day speeches—that something important had been missed. Or maybe that something important had been trivialized.

Motherhood is more than housework or cooking breakfast, no matter how a particular woman chooses to handle those day-to-day activities. On the other hand, motherhood is less than taking one hundred percent responsibility for the atmosphere of one's home, contrary to what I heard one Mother's Day speaker suggest. To imply that a mother can or should shoulder responsibility for the mood of an entire family flies in the face of agency and the choices that others in the family contribute.

So what does it really mean to be a "Mother in Israel"?

That is a brave question. Proceed with caution! For despite the kindly faced, apple-pie-and-apron-strings connotations, few subjects can engender more emotionally charged discussions with wider ranging ramifications, touching on everything from our lifestyles to the heart of our theology. And yet it is precisely because of this all-encompassing aspect that some clearer understanding of what it really means to be a Mother in Israel would be useful. But to be useful such an understanding will have to center on something larger than a particular household or cultural definition of motherhood. That's where most speeches and lessons on this subject have gone awry. But where can we find a perspective large enough to give a true balance to our view?

113

I turned to the scriptures.

If there is an answer, I think it lies in patterns—in noticing what God and the prophets have been saying about mothers over millennia of time. The focus is not on what any particular scripture says, but on what the body of scripture says consistently about motherhood. And the answer is interesting, both for what the sacred texts do and do not suggest.

Our uniquely Mormon scriptures—the Book of Mormon, Pearl of Great Price, and Doctrine and Covenants offer almost no references to motherhood. Section 68:25 addresses both fathers and mothers when it says "inasmuch as parents have children in Zion" and then goes on to admonish the teaching of correct principles. However, the section offers no advice on how to carry out that responsibility. The Bible, particularly the Old Testament, offers a number of interesting references. Though these references do not provide an exact definition of motherhood, they repeat some counsel again and again, which can be arranged into discernable patterns that provoke thought.

For example the influence of queen mothers is repeatedly acknowledged in the historical accounts of ancient Israel. The king's name is almost always followed by his mother's name and a brief description as to whether the king "did evil" or "walked in righteousness." The text seems to suggest a connection between the mother's influence and the king's quality of leadership. Twice the comment is more direct. King Asa is said to have removed his mother from court because of her bad influence (1 Kgs. 15:13; 2 Chron. 15:16), and King Ahaziah's unrighteousness is described as "walking in the way of his mother" (1 Kgs. 22:52). These queen mothers were seemingly involved in politics, most often religious politics. And their influence often led to the blessing or downfall of the whole Israelite nation.

> Most Israelite kings are introduced in scripture with the name of their mother and a description of their righteousness.
>
> Was that intended as a comment on the queen mother's influence?

KING	MOTHER	DESCRIPTION
Jeroboam	Zeruah	"lifted hand against king"
Rehoboam	Naamah	"did evil"
Abijam	Maachah	"walked in sins"
Asa	Maachah	"did right"
Jehoshaphat	Azubah	"walked in ways that were right"
Ahaziah	"he walked in the way of his mother"	"and caused Israel to sin"
Jehoram	"but not like his mother"	"wrought evil"
Ahaziah	Athaliah	"did evil"
Jehoash	Zibiah	"did right"
Amaziah	Johoaddan	"did right"
Azariah	Jecholiah	"did right"
Jotham	Jerusha	"did right"
Hezekiah	Abi	"did right"
Manasseh	Hephzibah	"did evil"
Amon	Meshullemeth	"did evil"
Josiah	Jedidath	"did right"
Jehoahaz	Hamutal	"did evil"
Jehoiakim	Zebudah	"did evil"
Jehoiachin	Nehushta	"did evil"
Zedekiah	Hamutal	"did evil"

One of the most interesting uses of the term *Mother in Israel* is in connection with Deborah, the prophetess (Judg. 4, 5). It would seem that she preferred to be called a Mother in Israel over all her other titles. She was the chief judge, or head of state. She was also a prophetess. She held these offices at a time when her nation was being harassed by a Canaanite army and paying onerous taxes to a foreign king.

As head of the Israelite nation, she was entitled to revelation to help her direct the affairs of her country. God revealed to her how the Canaanite army could be destroyed. She sent for her military chief and explained the battle strategy, assuring her commander that he could also count on God to aid in the struggle against their oppressors. Her military chief did as she commanded, and God sent a storm that mired the Canaanites in mud so thick they had to abandon their chariots. The result was that Deborah ruled over Israel for forty years of peace and prosperity. But when she sat down to write about her accomplishments, she began her account, "I Deborah arose . . . a mother in Israel" (Judg. 5:7).

There is also a story of a woman who stopped an army by asking its leader how he dared come against a Mother in Israel (2 Sam. 20:16–2). Her name isn't mentioned. She is simply called the Wise Woman of Abel. *Wise woman* is a term similar to *prophetess* (see chapter 2). It indicated a woman of influence and position, but like Deborah, this woman didn't call herself a wise woman. She called herself a Mother in Israel.

Joab, King David's commander-in-chief, surrounded the city of Abel with the intention of battering down the walls and destroying the people because they were harboring a man he thought was a traitor. As his soldiers were pounding on the city gates, a "wise woman" climbed onto the walls and called out to Joab, citing the accomplishments of her city and the fact that her people were known to be law abiding. Her town had been a source of peacemakers in the province—a fact she pointed out to Joab as proof that the city was too valuable for him to destroy. Then growing eloquent, she cried, "I am one of them that are peaceable and faithful . . . thou seekest to destroy a city and a mother in Israel." Following this woman's wise counsel the dispute was resolved, and Joab turned his army away, leaving the city of Abel at peace.

The way Deborah and the Wise Woman of Abel used their title Mother in Israel suggests that anciently motherhood commanded particular rights. Other scriptures support that notion. For example, Abraham never presumed to violate his wife Sarah's authority over their household (see Gen. 16:6), not even when that authority concerned her handmaid Hagar and the child Abraham had fathered by her. In fact, in matters concerning that child, Abraham was counseled by God to listen and to obey his wife (Gen. 21:12).

Moses encoded a concern for motherhood into his law. He commanded his followers to honor their fathers and mothers. But more importantly, he framed his legal code in such a way as to make the family central, and that was unusual. In antiquity the main purpose of government was generally regarded as conquest. War was the normal condition. The state was commonly little more than an armed camp under marital law, with the interests of the family hardly considered. The laws of Moses, by contrast, focused on the needs of peaceful communities made up of landholders devoted to agriculture and domestic life. One of the most striking examples is Deuteronomy 24:5: "When a man hath taken a new wife he shall not go out to war, neither shall he be charged with any business; but he shall be free at home one year, and shall cheer up his wife which he hath taken."

Today, coming from a background based on British legal

codes and their concern for providing a male heir, most Americans reading that law assume that Moses' intention was similar—that every man should have a son to carry on his name. But a careful reading of the scriptures suggests that while providing an heir was a factor, the ancients also felt strongly that it was wrong to deny a woman her children.

Marriage laws in Israel reflected this concern. As I have stated, if a woman married and her husband died before she had any children, the law said she was to be married to her husband's brother that she might have children by him (Deut. 25:5–6). Again at first glance the law seems to favor the husband—ensuring his continued posterity. It did. But in many cases it was the woman who sought to enforce this law.

117

A sense of how keenly the ancients felt about a woman's right to her children illuminates the odd story I told earlier of Tamar (see Gen. 38) and prompted Naomi's words to her daughters-in-law, Ruth and Orpah: "Turn again my daughters, why will ye go with me? Are there any more sons in my womb that they may be your husbands?" (Ruth 1:11). No matter how much Naomi loved the younger women, she had no more sons who could father their children.

Likewise the giving of Leah as wife to Jacob ahead of her younger sister, Rachel, was explained as a binding custom. "It must be so done in our country," Laban told his son-in-law (Gen. 29:26), suggesting how unthinkable it was to not provide a daughter with a husband and the means of her obtaining the blessings of having children.

It was this desire to possess the blessings and rights of motherhood that animated the prayers and consuming desires of the many barren women whose stories are told in the Bible. Sarah, Abraham's wife, wanted a child so badly she was willing to have it through her handmaid. Rebekah wrestled with the Lord because of her barrenness. Rachel wanted to die if she couldn't be a mother, and Elisabeth who is described as "righteous before God, walking in all the commandments. . ." (Luke 1:6).

Surely chief among these women was Eve who desired motherhood enough to risk mortality. In the book of Moses, she states plainly her understanding of what she had taken upon herself: "Were it not for our transgression, we never should have had seed" (Moses 5:11).

Anciently if a woman was clean and pure, she expected to be blessed with children. If children didn't come, she and others often interpreted that as a sign of shame or God's displeasure. Moses had promised that no one who kept the commandments would be barren (see Deut. 7:13–14). A righteous woman who was childless was placed in the same position as Job. Her friends and family would question what secret sin she must be harboring. In turn, she would become almost desperate in her feelings.

And so the scriptures describe the barren woman Hannah praying so fervently on the steps of the temple that the prophet Eli mistook her emotion for drunkenness and reproved her. "No, my lord," Hannah answered him, "Count not thine handmaid for a daughter of Belial [a popular name for Satan]" (1 Sam. 1:15–16). In essence Hannah's whole prayer expressed the same idea. She begged the Lord to take away her reproach—her worthlessness (an idea also expressed in the word *Belial*)—and give her the blessing of motherhood.

But the story of Hannah illustrates another important concept connected to motherhood as it has been preserved in scripture from ancient times. In her prayer Hannah promised the Lord that if she was given a manchild, she would return him to the temple to serve there. She made that covenant without first consulting with her husband and seemingly without fear that he would countermand it.

Other stories confirm that mothers made decisions affecting young children—a responsibility of motherhood recognized repeatedly by the Lord. A pattern emerges. Often when revelation needed to be communicated regarding young children, babes, or a child yet to be born, the mothers received the information first, and then later the fathers received a confirmation. This is not a pattern that holds true for older children—those probably over the age of twelve—but it is true of young children in example after example. In other words, the ancients not only held motherhood as sacred but also a woman's decisions concerning young children and childbearing. The most obvious example concerns Mary the Mother of the Savior. An angel appeared and told her she would be the most blessed woman among women. Later Joseph was told not to fear taking Mary as his wife.

An angel also appeared to a woman known only as Manoah's wife. The angel promised her a child and then asked her to live as a Nazarite, not drinking wine or any strong drink and not eating any unclean thing, that her child might be known as a Nazarite from the womb. The angel further instructed her to never allow a razor to touch her child's hair, explaining that his hair would be the source of his great strength. Her child, of course, was to be the Israelite champion Samson.

Manoah's wife agreed to follow the instructions of the angel. Then with great happiness she went and told her husband. He prayed that he might also be instructed, and the Lord answered the father's prayer by again sending an angel to the woman (Judg. 13:9). At this second visitation, the woman asks the angel to wait while she goes and gets her husband. When they are both present, the angel confirms the instructions he had previously given the wife.

Hagar, Sarah's bondwoman, is another good example of a mother who received the revelation she needed to guide her child's life. In fact, Hagar received revelation for her son even after he had grown to an age when the father usually took over, but by that time she had been sent away, divorced from Abraham's household, and left to rear her child alone (see Gen. 21:17–19, 21). Given those circumstances she seems to have assumed the role of both father and mother in receiving divine direction. An angel appears to Hagar and tells her how to save her child, who was very likely over the age of twelve, and tells her what blessings will come to the child—usually patriarchal privileges. Also Genesis 21:21 states, "and his mother took him a wife out of the land of Egypt"—a role usually played by the father.

There are other examples of women receiving revelation about the birth or rearing of their young children. Jochebed, Moses' mother, took such care in the construction of the basket she launched onto the river, she must have had faith that her plan would succeed. Joseph Smith suggests that Pharaoh's daughter was inspired or divinely appointed to be the young child's protector (JST Gen. 50:29).

There is one notable exception to this pattern—the angel announcing the birth of John the Baptist to his father, Zacharias, as he officiated in the temple. But later Elisabeth, John's mother, is filled with the Holy Ghost at the sound of her cousin Mary's salutation and knows that Mary is carrying the Lord. Who knows what revelation Elisabeth might have received concerning her own child. Perhaps the incident in the temple with Zacharias was the confirmation, not the announcement.

When Joseph Smith restored the gospel in this dispensation, he greatly increased the scriptures referring to Eve. He corrected or expanded other scriptural references to women and revived the term Mother in Israel. On several occasions he referred to his own mother using those words. Although, like the Bible, Joseph Smith never outlined a particular meaning for the phrase "Mother in Israel," he did encourage a broad role for women.

On one occasion, he described a visit he made to the Relief Society, saying: "I met the members of the Female

Relief Society, and after presiding at the admission of many
new members, gave a lecture on the priesthood, showing
how the sisters would come in possession of the privileges,
blessings, and the gifts of the priesthood, and that the signs
should follow them."[1]

In 1845 Brigham Young invited Lucy Mack Smith, the
Prophet's mother, to address a general conference. She
must have given a rousing speech for following her remarks,
Brigham Young stood and asked the congregation to give a
shout acclaiming her a Mother in Israel.[2]

The term is again used in a General Epistle from the
First Presidency dated 1856 which emphasized the importance of a mother being economically self-sufficient:
"Mothers in Israel, you are also called upon to bring up your
daughters to pursue some useful avocation for a sustenance,
that when they shall becomes [sic] the wives of Elders of
Israel, who are frequently called upon missions, or to devote
their time and attention to the things of the kingdom, they
may be able to sustain themselves and their offspring."[3]

The first baby blessed by the elders of the Church in
England, the infant daughter of James and Nancy Smithies,
was promised the blessings of a "mother in Israel."[4] Similarly
modern patriarchal blessings often promise a woman that
she will be a Mother in Israel or a Mother in Zion. And at
the dedication of the women's monument in Nauvoo, the
phrase "Mother in Israel" was used repeatedly.[5]

The Savior sometimes described his own role using
maternal imagery. Looking down upon Jerusalem shortly
before his death, he mourned, saying, "O Jerusalem,
Jerusalem, thou that killest the prophets, and stonest them
which are sent unto thee, how often would I have gathered
thy children together, even as a hen gathereth her chickens
under her wings, and ye would not!" (Matt. 23:37). Jesus
used the same image when he spoke to the Nephites (3 Ne.
10:4–6) and again repeatedly when he spoke to Joseph

Smith (D&C 10:65; 29:2; 43:24). Likewise, King David had prophesied many years earlier that the Savior would spread his wings over his people as a mother hen (Ps. 91:4).

Jesus Often Described Himself as a Mother Hen Gathering Her Chicks	David and Isaiah Also Saw Him That Way
Matthew 23:37	Psalms 91:4
Luke 13:34	Isaiah 8:8
3 Nephi 10:4-6	
D&C 10:65; 29:2; 43:24	

Mothering is often used in scripture to express spiritual dimensions. Moses cried unto the Lord when he was feeling the strain of his responsibilities and described his burden as trying to carry his people "as a nursing father beareth the sucking child" (Num. 11:12). Isaiah describes the Lord as saying, "Now will I cry like a travailing woman" (Isa. 42:14) and later reassures Israel by asking, "Can a woman forget her sucking child, that she should not have compassion on the son of her womb? yea, they may forget, yet will I not forget thee" (Isa. 49:15). In the Book of Mormon, Jacob repeatedly refers to "the mother tree" in his parable of the tame and wild olive trees (Jacob 5). And Jesus likened being converted to being born again.

Being spiritually renewed was the very essence of the higher law Jesus taught. He gave that concept substance by saying, "Except a man be born again . . ." (John 3:3). How do men and women overcome the world and prepare to receive the higher order? They must be reborn through the grace made possible by the Savior's sacrifice; they must progress from one state to another to achieve that new life. That progression does not come easily. None of us avoid causing others pain, ourselves suffering, or a need for repentance. But many of us also experience the joy of self-discovery and the renewal that follows repentance. The physical parallels to the spiritual change implied in that metaphor of a rebirth are all appropriate. Yet given the Jewish view of birth as a special source of impurity (they believed that a new mother was unclean seven days and subject to thirty-three days of purification, double if the child was a girl, another so-called "vessel of impurity"), Jesus' choice of that image as the central metaphor for his teaching about the higher spiritual laws seems surprising.

In light of Jewish feelings about birth, however, it is not surprising that when Jesus presented that concept to Nicodemus, a member of the Sanhedrin, he evidenced confusion, asking, "Can a man enter again into his mother's womb?"

Jesus did not glamorize the birth process. He did not speak of birth in terms of a woman's punishment or her salvation. He presented the image graphically, "a woman when she is in travail hath sorrow . . ." True spiritual conversion requires working through, laboring, overcoming and setting aside sin. Yet the birth-conversion process is positive. It leads to triumph. Jesus explained the process by saying "as soon as she is delivered of the child, she remembereth no more the anguish for joy" (John 16:21). What could better describe the Savior's concept of spirituality?

Yet there are still those who profess a darker view of motherhood. Some have interpreted the pangs of childbirth as a curse—the legacy of our mother Eve to all women. Others interpret Paul's first letter to Timothy as implying that only through childbirth can a woman be saved. Even some enlightened by restored scripture read D&C 132 and think that motherhood is a requirement for exaltation and/or the sole definition of a woman's eternal role.

Even if we don't understand all of what motherhood

means, the scriptures are clear on one point: Motherhood is a blessing with multifaceted spiritual dimensions. A blessing is never a duty, requirement, obligation, or curse. A blessing is something to be desired, freely accepted, a source of joy.

When Manoah's wife was asked by an angel to give up certain foods and strong drink that her child, Samson, might be known as a "Nazarite from the womb," she was given a choice. Mary was asked if she would accept the honor of being the most "blessed of all women." Even the Lord never assumes; he always asks. The choice is up to the woman.

While both historical and prophetic scriptures offer evidence enough to suggest there are blessings and rights associated with motherhood that are not currently appreciated or fully realized, it must also be acknowledged that those same blessings come with high expectations. Being a Mother in Israel implies rearing righteous offspring. That has never been easy.

124

Eve had lived in the Garden of Eden. She had walked and talked with God. She knew the tempter first hand. Even after she and Adam had been expelled from the Garden, she heard God's voice, listened, and obeyed (Moses 5:4–5). The scriptures say that a knowledge of God was one of the first things Eve taught her sons and daughters (Moses 5:12), but after the Fall she encountered a difficulty in her ability to teach spiritual truths. The things that had happened in the Garden were only stories to her children. Some believed and some didn't. That is the challenge that still complicates motherhood.

And surprisingly few scriptures beyond the few that advise "sparing the rod will spoil the child" (Prov. 13:24; 22:15) offer much concrete advice on how to go about instilling spiritual values into the next generation. Women are left to their motherly instincts, prayer, and a flow of personal revelation. Fortunately, the scriptures give examples of mothers successfully relying on exactly those sources. That is the comfort and quiet assurance the scriptures offer women who take on the responsibility of motherhood.

Perhaps all of us would do well to step back and take in that broader perspective from time to time, acknowledging not only the Lord's apparent confidence in mothers, but his deep involvement in their day-to-day responsibilities. It might give humility to our discussions of this topic.

Notes

1 Joseph Smith as quoted in Edward W. Tullidge, *The Women of Mormondom* (New York: 1877); photo lithographic reprint of original edition issued Salt Lake City, Utah, 1975, p. 489.

2 See Joseph Smith, *The History of The Church of Jesus Christ of Latter-day Saints* (Salt Lake City: Deseret Book, 1980), 7:470.

3 "Fourteenth General Epistle of the Presidency of The Church of Jesus Christ of Latter-day Saints," 10 December 1856, in James R. Clark, comp., *Messages of the First Presidency,* 6 vols. (Salt Lake City: Bookcraft, 1965-1975), 2:208-9.

4 See Edward W. Tullidge, *Women of Mormondom,* p. 245.

5 See speeches as reported in *Ensign,* January, 1979.

125

Even the Least of My Sisters
in the Scriptures

Eve, Sarah, Rebekah, Ruth, and Esther, each struggled and conquered. Their examples give oil to the lamps of those who follow. But for every Eve, Sarah, Rebekah, Ruth and Esther, thousands of other women met the same challenges unsung. Their examples, if noticed at all, are woven into the background of the scriptural narrative.

That should not be surprising. Most men and women in any age live quiet lives, making private decisions about their personal righteousness. Most are barely aware of the power with which their personal decisions may ripple through generations of their children, building or tearing at the foundations of Zion. However, those daily personal decisions are never overlooked by God, even if not recorded in the sacred accounts. And a suggestion of the power of the people en masse to accept or reject righteousness forms the backbone of all that the scriptures have to say.

Consider the crowds of women who followed Jesus. At first glance, they seem only a colorful backdrop for the more dramatic events. But it was the crowds who testified most often of him.

As Jesus entered Jerusalem for the last time, people lined the streets shouting, "Blessed be the King." They were using his correct title, for they knew who he was. But the Pharisees, who knew him not, rebuked Jesus and suggested that it would be more seemly if he asked his followers to be quiet. He replied, "If these should hold their peace, the stones would immediately cry out" (Luke 19:40).

Likewise, the nameless woman who washed the Savior's feet with her hair knew him when the host, in whose house

Jesus was a guest, did not (see Luke 7:36–50). It was Jesus' female followers, most of them nameless, who did not abandon him during his trial and crucifixion when even his apostles feared for their lives and Peter denied him. Earlier the support of these women had made the continuation of his work possible. Officials, afraid of Jesus' popularity, had left him alone for a time.

Jesus acknowledged the hundreds of private determinations for righteousness that these crowds represented. He referred to himself as their servant, and he was taking upon himself the sins of the world in service to every one of them and us. And when he taught, he did not generally enter into grand synagogues, universities, or palaces. Even at the temple in Jerusalem, he sat in the court of the women where everyone who wanted to hear could come.

One day, Jesus' apostles were disputing amongst themselves as to which of them was the greatest. That seems a petty question: Am I greater than you? I suspect, however, that too often that same notion haunts us, spilling out into our worry about the size and niceness of our houses, the model and newness of our cars . . . So it was with the apostles.

In the midst of that disputation, Salome, the mother of James and John, knelt before Jesus and requested that he place her sons to his right and left in his coming kingdom. In other words, she was asking the positions of greatest honor for her family.

How did Jesus answer her? "Whomsoever will be chief among you, let him be your servant" (Matt. 20:27).

The Savior meant it. He wasn't saying that some people should be humble because we can't all be leaders. He meant that if we would be leaders, effective workers in his kingdom, then we must be servants. But how must we serve?

Jesus healed Peter's mother-in-law so she could get up and fix a meal. Obviously a meal was needed, not a prayer

127

or a sermon. Similarly Jesus spoke of women busy at grindstones as an example of women's day-to-day activities.
Earlier the prophet Jeremiah warned of a time when "I will
take from thee the sound of the millstones . . . and the
whole land shall be a desolation (Jer. 25:10–11), meaning
that such homey activities were a sign of good fortune, for
when the millstones fell silent it meant famine in the land.

On the other hand, Martha of Bethany, bustling about
her kitchen, suffered another kind of famine—a famine of
the spirit. She let resentment build until she was angry at
her sister and worse, angry at Jesus for letting Mary sit at his
feet. "Lord, dost thou not care that my sister hath left me to
serve alone?" (Luke 10:40).

Clearly she was conscientious and hardworking. As such,
her service was fine and no doubt appreciated, but her attitude needed to be improved. Being a good servant means
more than keeping the millstones turning. Any service ren-
dered unwillingly is drudgery. There is a time to cook and
clean and a time to sit at the Master's feet and learn.

Later when Mary anointed the Savior with costly oil,
her service distressed the apostles with its extravagance.
They felt the oil would have been better sold and the poor
helped with the money. But Jesus accepted her gift and
praised her for it. More than oil, her gift was homage—a
personal acknowledgement of Jesus as Lord and Savior.

Paul praised two Roman women named Tryphena and
Tryphosa, early members of the Christian Church (Rom.
16:12). He praised them for their tireless service. We know
from other historical accounts that Tryphena was a member
of the royal Roman family and prominent at court.
Presumably Tryphosa was, too. More interesting is that Paul
describes both of these women as having their names in the
Book of Life. Then he goes on to urge these women to
resolve some difference that is causing a division within the
Roman branch of the Church.

I learn two things from that: one, we do not all have to be alike or even to agree with one another to be right-eous—to have our names in the Book of Life—and two, that we cannot let our differences divide us. We need one another. We need to give and receive one another's service. The kingdom of God is a community effort.

The fact that the Lord watches over, protects, and has purposes for all nations of the earth is confirmed repeat-edly by the prophets. In the Old Testament the Lord states, "Are ye not as the children of the Ethiopians unto me, O children of Israel? saith the Lord. . . . and the Philistines from Caphtar, and the Syrians from Kir?" (Amos 9:7). In the Book of Mormon God says, "I remember one nation like unto another" (2 Ne. 29:8).

This is true of individuals as well. The Lord respects and honors each of us with wonderful promises. Those who serve faithfully in even the most humble circumstances have been promised powers, principalities, and dominions. We shall be queens and priestesses. Perhaps the greatest words that any of us will ever hear are: "Well done thou good and faithful servant." But sometimes we forget the rest of that scripture: "Well done thou good and faithful servant: thou has been faithful over a few things . . ." (Matt. 25:21).

I am in a particularly hectic stage of life with a house full of teenagers, teaching assignments, church callings. Your circumstances may be different, but with the same effect. Most of us live busy lives. We hope all our work, worry, and bustle has some effect—that we're being faithful over a few things.

Unfortunately there have been times in my life when I have put in full days doing everything for everybody on everyone else's schedule thinking that I was rendering ser-vice. I know other sisters who feel that others will not love them, or, worse, that the Lord cannot love them if they don't spend themselves in that kind of continuous serving.

129

Too many of my sisters too literally lose themselves in this false sacrificial role. They become caretakers or rescuers and never find their own identity. This is not service. This is not what the Savior meant when he said, "He that loses himself will find himself." One finds oneself in service only when it is given willingly, even delightfully. Anything else is coercion, and we all know who is the author of coercion. Maybe it's time to repent. Time to return to holy ground and become complete. Christ said we should be servants. He did not say that we could never ask anything for ourselves. In fact, we must ask whatever is needed to make us the best servants possible. That requires balance and enough sense of self to know what we need and how to get it.

130

My suggestion: Read closer . . . closer . . . and closer yet. Read until you notice not only Sarah, Rebekah, Ruth and Esther, but also the women in the crowds around Jesus. Read until you see the women in those crowds not only gazing upon Jesus with admiration, but as vitally involved in his work, essential support.

One reason I care about my sisters in the scriptures is that when my focus gets fine enough, even the nameless crowds inspire and enlighten me. What better examples of service?

MAKING THE
SCRIPTURES OUR OWN

I was teaching a gospel doctrine class on the eight witnesses of the Book of Mormon when someone raised the question of why no women were given a chance to see the gold plates? Someone else in the class responded that women were never called to "witness."

I mentioned at that point that the first witnesses of Christ's resurrection were all women. Of particular interest is Mark's account. In chapter 16, an angel greets the women, testifies of Christ's resurrection, and then shows the women the tomb in a manner not unlike the way the angel showed the gold plates to the three witnesses of the Book of Mormon.[1] In Matthew's account (chapter 28), after the angel commands the women to "go quickly and tell his disciples" (v. 7), the women are met on their way by Jesus himself, who invites them to feel his feet and hands and then repeats the angel's command: "Go tell my brethren" (v. 10).

As I continued the lesson, I found that no one was aware that David Whitmer's mother was shown the gold plates by the angel Moroni.[2] Nor were they familiar with Emma Smith's account of a time when she felt the plates through a thin wrapper. She talks of the size of the plates and the feel of the hinges. She mentions running her finger up the edge and the distinctive rustle that the gold pages made. We know Joseph Smith's sister Katherine also held the gold plates, again with the plates being wrapped in a light covering. Joseph Smith's mother wrote of another time when her son came in and handed her the Urim and Thummim and let her examine them.[3] These women's accounts give us far more physical detail of those artifacts than anything written by the official eight witnesses.

I had a similar experience teaching a Christmas lesson in Relief Society one time. I discovered that the women in my class had only one mental picture of Mary, the mother of the Savior. They saw her as the young mother holding the baby Jesus. They were unaware of the contributions she made throughout Christ's life, nor did they realize how involved she was with the apostles following Christ's death and resurrection. They did not know that Mary and sev-eral other women were present at the Pentecost when the Holy Ghost descended upon Christ's disciples (Acts 1:14).

I often encounter women who bemoan the lack of scriptural references to women. I sympathize. I, too, have ached to know my foremothers better and indulged feelings of frustration at what I thought was a lack. But lately my concern has shifted. The scriptural references to women may be few, but I wish more of my sisters and brothers appreciated what is available.

Have we plumbed the significance of the women who first saw the resurrected Christ? Do we fully understand the calling of Christ's mother, Mary? Are we aware of the contributions of Joseph Smith's sisters and mother? Is it fair to ask for more before we embrace what we have?

But it goes deeper than that. If we read insisting that we must find what we think ought to be there, we will be in danger of missing the message—what the Lord is trying to tell us. And what the Lord is trying to tell us is always very personal. But to reach that level of understanding, the reader must put something of herself into the study.

The scriptures, after all, are only words until we interact with them. No matter how many stories we read illustrating how God's word has transformed individuals, even whole nations, those stories will remain only stories until we add our own. Reading scripture and then writing a journal response is one way to do this.

The act of writing requires participation, and reading a particular scripture may trigger a number of responses: a feeling, a question, a memory. As we explore the personal implications of a particular passage, we cannot help but create a touchstone for testimony. We become involved; we quicken ancient words and make them alive anew.

But most people don't consider themselves "writers." In fact, for many just thinking about writing can conjure up all the anxieties associated with high school term papers. However, a private journal is whatever we make it. Writing does not have to be "literature" to clarify, focus, and provide a larger understanding of self. As every individual is unique, so every journal will be unique.

133

A scripture journal is not the same as a simple diary. It is the chronicle of a spiritual odyssey. Some pages may sing God's praises, acknowledging the wonder and beauty of creation or answered prayers or sudden insights. Other entries may consist of anguished questions about suffering—our own or that observed in the world. The journal may include expressions of doubts and incomplete understandings as well as deeper discernings and records of spiritual enlightenment too precious to share with any but our most intimate of associates—all of which document the spiritual undergirding of our life.

The scripture journal is a place to take stock. In the process, it may be the place where kindled faith fans into a personal "burning bush." In the end that's what we really want. Yes, more passages of scripture specifically about women would be nice, but more personal faith and testimony is even better. When we put forth the effort to make the scriptures our own, we cannot but discover their abundance and enlarge ourselves in the process.

How to Do a Scripture Journal

There is no "right way" to keep a scripture journal. It's not necessary to write every day or to do a certain number of pages or to try to give careful, scholarly analysis. You only need look inward and write honestly. But the following hints may be helpful:

1. Find a quiet place and clear your mind.

2. Pray.

3. Read the passage and try to visualize what is being presented.

4. Check any confusing words in the Bible Dictionary or other reference.

5. Read again and jot down ideas that come to you. You may want to ponder the passage—or meditate.

6. Open your journal and write. Let your writing flow naturally. Spelling and grammar don't matter. Searching your true feelings and writing honestly do matter. Capture what comes to your mind.

You may want to date your entries. That way you will be able to see how your ideas on a particular scripture change from time to time. The important thing is to feel free to use the scripture journal in whatever way seems most comfortable. A scripture journal is a gift of space and time that we give ourselves in order to discover our own feelings and take measure of our own spirituality.

To help you get started, consider the following passages and questions, which all refer to women in one way or another. Together they represent a good sample of what the scriptures have to offer women, specifically, that is uplifting, stimulating, and pertinent. Arranged in no particular order, the suggested passages can be explored at will, discovering those scriptures that speak most clearly first, perhaps returning over and over to a particular passage, maybe wandering far afield using the suggested topical guide headings.

In any case, this is only a beginning. Once in the habit, you can continue choosing your own course, selecting your own passages.

#1

> And now, he imparteth his word by angels unto men, yea, not only men but women also. Now this is not all; little children do have words given unto them many times, which confound the wise and the learned.
> Alma 32:23

135

Who was Alma addressing when he said the angels impart the word of God to men, women and even little children? What prompted his words?

On another occasion, Jesus told his followers that they would recognize the true Church by the signs that would follow those who believed (see Mark 16:17–18). In yet other circumstances Moses wished "that all the Lord's people were prophets and that the Lord would put his spirit upon them" (see Num. 11:29).

Do you know stories of individuals, even little children, who have "received the word of God"? Have members of your family?

What about you? How many different ways have you received inspiration? How have you known when it was from God?

See Topical Guide Headings: Holy Ghost, Inspiration, Inspire, Source of Testimony

#2

*And Eve, his wife, heard all these things and was glad,
saying: Were it not for our transgressions we never should
have had seed, and never should have known good and
evil, and the joy of our redemption, and the eternal life
which God giveth unto all the obedient.*

*And Adam and Eve blessed the name of God, and they
made all things known unto their sons and their daughters.*
   Moses 5:11–12

*Among the great and mighty ones who were assembled in
this vast congregation of the righteous were Father Adam,
the Ancient of Days, and father of all,*

*And our glorious Mother Eve, with many of her faithful
daughters who had lived through the ages and worshiped
the true and living God.*
   D&C 138:38–39

136

How do you feel about your mother Eve? Does the fact that
she is with her faithful daughters in the next world give
you a sense of excitement? Do you feel that you might meet
and work with her some time? Can you imagine meeting
her?

Why was Eve glad? What is there in the midst of our
fallen condition—mortality and an imperfect world—for
which we, like Eve, might rejoice?

Eve risked much that her children might be born and
that she and they might have the greater knowledge of
good and evil. What have you learned about good and evil?
Have you experienced that knowledge as bittersweet?
Could it have been otherwise?

What do you owe your mother Eve? If you could write
her a letter, what might you say?

See Bible Dictionary: Eve

#3

And, behold, there was a woman which had a spirit of infirmity eighteen years, and was bowed together, and could in no wise lift up herself.

And when Jesus saw her, he called her to him, and said unto her, Woman thou art loosed from thine infirmity.

And he laid his hands on her: and immediately she was made straight, and glorified God.

And the ruler of the synagogue answered with indignation, because that Jesus had healed on the sabbath day, and said unto the people, There are six days in which men ought to work: in them therefore come and be healed, and not on the sabbath day.

The Lord then answered him, and said, Thou hypocrite, doth not each one of you on the sabbath loose his ox or his ass from the stall, and lead him away to watering?

And ought not this woman, being a daughter of Abraham, whom Satan hath bound, lo, these eighteen years, be loosed from this bond on the sabbath day?

And when he had said these things, all his adversaries were ashamed: and all the people rejoiced for all the glorious things that were done by him.

Luke 13:11–17

This passage is often cited in discussions about appropriate activities for the Sabbath day, but note the respect Jesus gives the woman, referring to her as "a daughter of Abraham." Contrast that to the attitude of the ruler of the synagogue who seems to suggest the woman is at fault for even attracting her Savior's attention: "There are six days in which men ought to work: in them . . . come and be healed."

How does that make you feel about yourself? About your Savior? About the worth and dignity of all God's children? About your own attitude toward the poor, the sick, the infirm, or the less fortunate?

Have you ever felt treated as less than "a daughter of Abraham"? Do you ever allow such treatment to affect your own sense of self-worth?

See Topical Guide Heading: Worth of Souls

#4

> *And he said . . . Sarah thy wife shall have a son. And Sarah heard it in the tent door, which was behind him.*
>
> *Now Abraham and Sarah were old and well stricken in age; and it ceased to be with Sarah after the manner of women.*
>
> *Therefore Sarah laughed within herself . . . .*
>
> *And the Lord said unto Abraham, Wherefore did Sarah laugh, saying, Shall I of a surety bear a child, which am old?*
>
> *Is any thing too hard for the Lord?*
>
> Gen. 18:10–14

Is anything too hard for the Lord?

Sarah "laughed" because she had given up hoping for a child. It must have seemed to her that having grown old without a child meant that her many petitions for posterity had been denied. Do you have righteous desires you have given up praying for?

Sarah received her child. Do you know stories of modern miracles? Of answered prayers? Have you experienced such yourself? Was there a feeling of surprise—"laughter"—at the recognition of that miracle?

Sarah gave birth to Isaac, but did that end her trials? Are you ever tempted to think that if only one thing were different then your troubles would be over? Realistically imagine how it might be if some long unanswered prayer were suddenly answered. How would your life be different? What new challenges would you face? Do you believe it can happen? Will happen?

See Topical Guide Headings: Miracle; Supplication

#5

> *Then Mordecai commanded to answer Esther, Think not with thyself that thou shalt escape in the king's house, more than all the Jews.*
>
> *For if thou altogether holdest thy peace at this time, then shall . . . deliverance arise to the Jews from another place; but thou and thy father's house shall be destroyed: and who knoweth whether thou art come to the kingdom for such a time as this?*
>
> *Then Esther bade them return Mordecai this answer,*
>
> *Go, gather together all the Jews that are present in Shushan, and fast ye for me, and neither eat nor drink three days, night or day: I also and my maidens will fast likewise; and so will I go in unto the king, which is not according to the law: and if I perish, I perish.*
>
> *Esther 4:13–16*

You remember the story. The Jews had been condemned to death. Esther was the queen and a Jew, but the king was unaware of her family background. It had been kept a secret. Her uncle sent to her asking her to intercede in behalf of her people. It meant risking her life, but he argued that perhaps her mission in life was just that—to save her nation in their time of peril. "Who knoweth whether thou art come to the kingdom for such a time as this?" he asked.

Do you feel you have a particular mission in life?

Do you know women, like Esther, who have stepped up to a particular calling or who have dedicated themselves to an important undertaking? Do you admire them?

Esther prepared by fasting three days and asking all the Jews in Shushan to fast with her. What preparation does your mission require? How had Esther prepared herself long before her uncle's request? Is it possible to prepare yourself even before you know what your mission is? How?

See Topical Guide Heading: Mission of Latter-day Saints

#6

> *Hearken unto the voice of the Lord your God, while I speak unto you, Emma Smith, my daughter; for verily I say unto you, all those who receive my gospel are sons and daughters in my kingdom.*
>
> *A revelation I give unto you concerning my will; and if thou art faithful and walk in the paths of virtue before me, I will preserve thy life, and thou shalt receive an inheritance in Zion.*
>
> *Behold, thy sins are forgiven thee, and thou art an elect lady, whom I have called. . . .*
>
> *And thou shalt be ordained under his hand to expound scriptures, and to exhort the church, according as it shall be given thee by my Spirit.*
>
> *For he shall lay his hands upon thee, and thou shalt receive the Holy Ghost, and thy time shall be given to writing, and to learning much.*
>
> *D&C 25: 1–3, 7–8*

Section 25 records a blessing that was given to Emma Smith shortly before her twenty-sixth birthday. She had lost a baby and found herself estranged from her family because of her husband's religious activities. As if that weren't enough, just prior to receiving this blessing her own baptism had been disrupted by officials arresting her husband for disorderly conduct, and her confirmation had to be delayed. In these circumstances, she felt she needed a blessing and sought one.

Under the hands of her husband, the Lord comforted Emma and called her to specific and important tasks. As one intimate with her weaknesses, he also exhorted her. The words are kind, loving, exact, and startlingly personal.

How well does the Lord know you?

When and where have you received priesthood blessings? What have such blessings meant in your life?

See Topical Guide Heading: Hands, Laying on of

#7

The queen of the south shall rise up in the judgment with the men of this generation, and condemn them: for she came from the utmost parts of the earth to hear the wisdom of Solomon; and behold, a greater than Solomon is here.
Luke 11:31

The "queen of the south" is better known as the Queen of Sheba. Although her journey to see Solomon and test his legendary wisdom has been much romanticized, in this passage the Savior suggests that rather than having a love interest in a famous king, the woman had a genuine desire for greater knowledge. She came to see Solomon as a student wanting to learn. What's more, Jesus says that on the Judgment Day she will rise up and condemn those who fail to seek similar wisdom, especially those who failed to recognize the Savior and know that he could teach them all things.

141

Does the Savior's reference to this queen alter your view of her?

Do you know of other individuals who have made extraordinary efforts to find and embrace the truth? Have you?

How great is your desire for more light and knowledge? Where do you seek it? How do you know when you've found it?
See Topical Guide Heading: Wisdom

#8

To Timothy, my dearly beloved son: . . .
When I call to remembrance the unfeigned faith that is in thee, which dwelt first in thy grandmother Lois, and thy mother Eunice; and I am persuaded that in thee also.
2 Timothy 1:2, 5

. . . Yea, they had been taught by their mothers, that if they did not doubt, God would deliver them.

And they rehearsed unto me the words of their mothers,
saying: We do not doubt our mothers knew it.
  Alma 56:47–48

How can one person's faith come to dwell in another? How
does one become so sure of another's testimony as to be able
to say, "We do not doubt our mothers knew it"?

Have faith and testimonies been passed down in your
family? What can you do to start or continue such a tradition?

Are your friends, family, and associates aware of your
beliefs? Would any of them be willing to stand and say, "We
doubt not that she knew it"?

  See Topical Guide Heading: Testimony

142

#9

Enoch looked upon the earth; and he heard a voice from
the bowels thereof, saying: Wo, wo is me, the mother of
men; I am pained, I am weary, because of the wickedness
of my children. When shall I rest, and be cleansed from the
filthiness which is gone forth out of me? When will my
Creator sanctify me, that I may rest, and righteousness for
a season abide upon my face?
  Moses 7:48

Did Enoch actually hear the earth speak? Or is he express-
ing himself symbolically?

Many Eastern and Native American religions view the
earth as a living organism. Even in modern scientific cir-
cles, the "Gaia Hypothesis," which states that the earth
acts like a living entity and therefore ought to be regarded
as such, has been gaining more and more credence. Does
this scripture seem to agree?

In what way is the earth our mother? Have you ever felt
a kinship with the earth? Have you ever felt connected to
a particular place? Inspired by a particular nature scene?

In another scripture we are told: "And God blessed them [Adam and Eve], and said unto them, Be fruitful, and multiply and replenish the earth and subdue it" (Gen. 1:28). Is it significant that our first parents were commanded to replenish as well as subdue?

See Topical Guide Heading: Earth, Renewal of

#10

For behold, I, the Lord, have seen the sorrow, and heard the mourning of the daughters of my people in the land of Jerusalem, yea, and in all the lands of my people, because of the wickedness and abominations of their husbands.

And I will not suffer, saith the Lord of Hosts, that the cries of the fair daughters of this people, which I have led out of the land of Jerusalem, shall come up unto me against the men of my people, saith the Lord of Hosts.

For they shall not lead away captive the daughters of my people because of their tenderness, save I shall visit them with a sore curse, even unto destruction; . . .

Jacob 2:31–33

Likewise, ye husbands, dwell with them according to knowledge, giving honour unto the wife, as unto the weaker vessel, and as being heirs together of the grace of life; that your prayers be not hindered.

1 Peter 3:7

143

One of the hotter topics of our day is women's rights and the history of female oppression. But obviously the problem is not new if both Jacob and Peter found occasion to speak of it. But who were Jacob and Peter most worried about? The "daughters who mourn"? Or the "men of my people" in danger of a sore curse? Whose prayers may be hindered?

How does the debate on women's rights affect your spirituality? The Church's? The nation's? Is it more damaging to confront wrongs or live with them? How do you personally feel about these issues? Can you think of new ways to discuss this "age-old" problem that will be more healing? More enhancing to the spiritual growth for all concerned?

See Topical Guide Headings: Unrighteous Dominion; Woman, Women

#11

> (Yea, a sword shall pierce through thy own soul also,) . . .
> Luke 2:35

When Mary and Joseph brought the baby Jesus to the temple eight days after his birth, Simeon took the child in his arms and testified that he knew this was the Savior come into the world. Then he went on to prophesy concerning Jesus. These particular words foreshadow the soldier who would pierce the Savior's side with a sword as he hung on the cross but are meant to express sorrow, not for Jesus, but for Mary.

What was he saying about Mary's suffering at the cross and her own sacrifice? How was her experience like Abraham's? Like God the Father's?

What have you learned from the suffering of your children or those close to you? Is that different than what you've learned from your own suffering?

See Topical Guide Headings: Innocence, Innocent; Suffering

#12

> And Hannah prayed, and said, My heart rejoiceth in the Lord. . . .
>
> There is none holy as the Lord: for there is none beside thee: neither is there any rock like our God. . . .
>
> The Lord killeth, and maketh alive: he bringeth down to the grave, and bringeth up.
>
> The Lord maketh poor, and maketh rich: he bringeth low, and lifteth up.
>
> He raiseth up the poor out of the dust, and lifteth up the beggar from the dunghill, to set them among princes, and to make them inherit the throne of glory: for the pillars of

the earth are the Lord's, and he hath set the world upon them.

He will keep the feet of his saints, and the wicked shall be silent in darkness; for by strength shall no man prevail.

The adversaries of the Lord shall be broken to pieces; out of heaven shall he thunder upon them: the Lord shall judge the ends of the earth; and he shall give strength unto his king, and exalt the horn of his anointed.

1 Samuel 2:1–2, 6–10

In one of the most beautiful poems found in sacred text, Hannah describes her Lord as:

> *a rock*
> *one who makes alive*
> *one who lifts up the beggar*
> *one who keeps the feet of the saints*
> *and as thunder out of heaven.*

145

How would you describe your Lord? What phrases would you use?

See Bible Dictionary: Christ, Names of

Other Scriptures to Keep Your Journal Going

1 NEPHI 5:7–8 (SARIAH'S TESTIMONY)

Her sons had journeyed back to Jerusalem, were long overdue, and she feared they had perished. But when they returned, all her fears changed to joy. Then she knew "of a surety" that what they were undertaking as a family was right.

Have you experienced moments when you recognized the Lord directing your life?

See Topical Guide Heading: Guidance, Divine

LUKE 1:38

An angel appeared to Mary. As a young girl she couldn't have known all that was being asked of her; nevertheless, she embraced God's will.

In what ways have you embraced God's will?

See Topical Guide Heading: Will

MATTHEW 28:5–10

After the Sabbath following the Savior's crucifixion, several women who had been closely associated with Jesus came to his tomb. But they were met by an angel proclaiming the news that Jesus was not dead! He showed them the empty tomb and asked them to bear witness to what they'd seen.

But they were to see, hear, and feel an even greater thing. Jesus appeared to them, spoke to them, and let them touch his feet that they might truly know he was alive. Then he, too, urged the women to testify—to go and tell the brethren.

Thus they became the first witnesses to the miracle of the Resurrection.

Of what have you been asked to witness? What have you seen, heard, and felt of God that you dare not deny?

See Topical Guide Headings: Resurrection; Witness, Witnesses

DEUTERONOMY 5:16; PROVERBS 1:8; 6:20

The commandment to honor one's father and mother is given in scripture at least ten times. What is so important about giving respect to our parents that it should have been so often repeated?

While he was hanging on the cross, Jesus looked down and, seeing Mary, commanded John to care for her as though she were his mother. The scriptures say that "from that hour that disciple took her unto his own home" (see John 19:25–27).

What has your mother meant to you? How do you honor her?

See Topical Guide Heading: Honoring Father and Mother

LUKE 7:36–50

How is it that a woman who was a sinner knew that Jesus was the Christ when others, including a wealthy and renowned Pharisee, didn't?

Where did she get her sure knowledge? Have you sought the same knowledge? How and where did you look?

See Topical Guide Heading: Jesus Christ, Taking the Name of

JEREMIAH 6:2–7; MICAH 4:10

Zion is often personified in scripture in feminine symbols and referred to as the "Lamb's Bride" Why? What does that mean to you?

See Topical Guide Headings: Bride; Sion, Zion,

JOHN 4:10–15; ISAIAH 12:3

147

Jesus has offered you the same "living water." How have you answered him?

See Topical Guide Heading: Eternal Life

JST REVELATION 12:1–7; 12–17

A difficult passage full of symbolism and layers of meanings, and yet the images can be powerful. How is the Church like a woman delivering a child that must be hidden and protected? Satan is presented as a formidable foe, but the earth and angels help the woman. What's more, there is never any suggestion that Satan can or will prevail despite all his efforts. Do you take comfort in that?

Do you know women who have brought forth children and then gone to great lengths to protect them from Satan? Have you or anyone you know been aided by angels?

See Bible Dictionary: Revelation of John

JOSHUA 2:9–10; HEBREWS 11:31; JAMES 2:25

Rahab's story inspired scripture writers for hundreds, even thousands, of years. They refer to her as an example of faith and as an example of works.

What stories of faith have been handed down in your family? Do they still have the power to inspire?
See Topical Guide Heading: Faith

JOHN 16:21

Despite the fact that the Jews viewed childbirth as "unclean," Jesus used the image of giving birth on several occasions. He never glorified it, nor did he reduce it to the animal level. In this instance, he compares it to the sorrow of his leaving and the joy of his return.

How do you feel about the process of giving birth? Was bringing children forth in sorrow a necessary part of the Fall? Is it as Jesus describes: a moment of pain followed by a great joy?

What about childrearing? How are joy and sorrow mixed in that process? What joy can no man take from you? Can you imagine the joy of the Savior's return?
See Topical Guide Headings: Joy; Marriage, Motherhood.

MATTHEW 26:7–13

How does one give praise and honor to God? He has said repeatedly in scripture that what he wants from us is "a contrite heart." He also wants us to do his will, feed his poor, and comfort the sick. But when is that not enough? When is it appropriate to offer God "our best ointment"?
See Topical Guide Headings: Glorify; Praise.

GALATIANS 3:28; 2 NEPHI 26:33

Do you sincerely believe that "all are alike unto God"? How have you tried to put that belief into practice?

If all are "alike," does that mean we must love the sinner as well as the saint? The stranger as well as the sister? How does one love unconditionally? Is that easy?

Why do the scriptures repeatedly warn us "not to judge"? What is the danger of applying our own judgments?

Have you witnessed an act of unconditional love? What

impressed you about the incident? What made you remember it?

See Topical Guide Headings: Brotherhood and Sisterhood; Charity

ISAIAH 54:1

Do you believe that God is always fair? Always generous? Have you experienced times when you felt neglected by the Lord? Overlooked? Disappointed?

Have you ever been angry with him? Argued with him? Questioned him?

Here the Lord says that the barren (the disappointed) should break forth into singing and rejoice. Why? Is he promising that those who wait for their blessings will be blessed even more richly? But how comforting is that? If God's patience is endless, does that mean ours must be as enduring?

Have you or others you've known found reason to rejoice even in the face of disappointment? Was that easy? Worthwhile?

What have you learned from your times of personal "desolation"? In the end, were your blessings multiplied?

See Topical Guide Headings: Patience, Patient, Patiently ; Reward

ISAIAH 49:15

Throughout scriptures individuals, families, whole nations have repeatedly forgotten and forsaken their God. But he does not forsake them.

The Lord wants to be our God. He has said that it is his work and his glory to bring to pass the immortality and eternal life of his children (see Moses 1:39). That is his focus, his reason for being, and nothing can make him deviate from that purpose.

We deviate. Have there been times in your life when you felt forsaken and alone? When? Why? What experiences have you had with repentance? Have you returned to

God and found him? Have you felt the power of forgiveness? Do you truly believe he can never forget you?
See Topical Guide Heading: Forsake, Forsook, Forsaken

MOSIAH 27:25–26

How does the image of birth—being born again—help your understanding of the plan of salvation? What does it mean to become a new creature? Because of the gospel, have you ever felt changed? renewed? different?
See Topical Guide Headings: Conversion, Convert; Man, New, Spiritually Reborn

JOEL 2:28–29

What do you think it means to have the spirit poured out
upon all flesh?

Have you felt the spirit moving in the world today? Do you sense any part of this scripture being fulfilled in your life or the lives of those close to you?

Do you find these exciting times in which to live? Are you glad to be alive now? Many, many prophets anticipated the last days and envied those who would see their fulfillment. Do you share that anticipation?

Can you imagine a time when everyone—sons and daughters, old and young, the lofty and the humble—will be so filled with God's spirit that they will all prophesy? What will it be like to be alive then?
See Topical Guide Headings: Jesus Christ, Last Days, Millennial Reign

Notes

1. See Joseph Smith, *The History of The Church of Jesus Christ of Latter-day Saints* (Salt Lake City: Deseret Book, 1980), 1:54–55.
2. B.H. Roberts, *Comprehensive History of the Church* (Provo, Utah: Brigham Young University Press, 1965), 1:127.
3. There are multiple sources that describe how Joseph Smith's family members handled the plates. But see in particular Luck Mack Smith, *History of Joseph Smith by His Mother* (Salt Lake City: Bookcraft, 1979); or Linda King Newell and Valeen Tippetts Avery, *Mormon Enigma: Emma Hale Smith* (New York: Doubleday, 1984), 21.

GETTING FROM
EVERYDAY TO ETERNITY

My son and his friends turned 400 crickets loose in the school library. And got caught!

To him it was an issue of fairness. He and his friends had organized a band and were using one of the high school music rooms as a place to practice. Until the librarian complained. She said they were disturbing the students using the library after hours. My son pointed out with indignation that sixty-member marching bands played in that same music room during the school day. That didn't seem to disturb the students in regular study hall.

So feeling that the librarian didn't need to think she owned the school, and knowing she had a particular dislike for creepy, crawly things, my son and his friends went to the pet store and bought 400 crickets at a nickel apiece—the store's entire inventory. When the librarian turned her back, they dumped the crickets on the top of her desk. I didn't see it, but I'm told they swarmed over her desk, up the wall, onto some of the book stacks, and literally sent the librarian screaming into the hall.

By afternoon the school had closed the library and taped the doors shut in an effort to keep the crickets from spreading. Meanwhile, the crickets began to chirp. They could be heard all over the school. Which meant that soon the story of where these crickets had come from was also being heard all over the school. My son and his friends had become instant celebrities among the other students—famed for their "Cricket Caper." Everyone was talking about it, including the school administrators, who had decided they couldn't let these kids get away with this or they would never be able to exert any kind of control again. As a result they had decided to go for severe punishment—suspending the kids from school.

Things had gotten to that point before I heard anything about it. My reaction was a groan. What a mess! And I didn't really want to have to deal with it. Robert Frost expressed it aptly when he wrote, "Home is the place where when you go there, they have to take you in." My son had created a problem for himself, but when he brought it home, we had to help him with it because we were his family.

I think we have to call the situation what it was—vandalism. In fact, if the school had wanted to pursue it through legal channels, they could have charged my son and his friends with a misdemeanor. And it needs to be pointed out that if you have a problem with the school librarian or the school's policies concerning the use of the practice rooms after hours, dumping 400 crickets in the library is not the best way to handle that problem. You don't solve things by getting even. My son and his friends had not demonstrated any great degree of maturity— although I was willing to give them maybe half a point for creativity.

On the other hand, neither my son nor any of his friends had ever been in trouble at school before. In fact, my son had never even had so much as a tardy in a single class in three years at that school. Suspending him for a prank that had never been intended to be malicious and did little harm was too harsh. Although I could understand the administrator's position, I thought being fair was a better answer than being tough. Clearly the school was overreacting, and somebody needed to stand up for the kids.

It was interesting to see how the various families handled the situation. One father told his son he'd gotten himself into trouble, he could get himself out. Another family began yelling loudly in all directions, threatening to sue the administrators if their action traumatized their son or in any way jeopardized his continued education. At the same time, I'm told, they were threatening their son—telling him that they would kick him out of the house if he ever embarrassed them like that again. The other three families, including my own, sat down with their kids and the school administrators and talked out the problem until we arrived at an acceptable solution—namely that the boys and their families paid for an exterminator.

So what does this episode have to do with how studying the women in the scriptures has changed my life?

Family. Our connectedness, our close relationships are not just the haphazard, day-to-day jumble of our lives. Family is the link between everyday and eternity.

When my son came home from school and announced that he had turned 400 crickets loose in the school library, we then faced the challenge of helping him walk away from that situation a little wiser. Joseph Smith was the same age as my son when he came in from the woods one day and announced that he'd just seen a vision. I've come to appreciate how his family responded to that news.

His was an interesting family, a large family full of strong, diverse personalities—most of them tending to be free-thinking individuals. Let me remind you that Joseph Smith was only fourteen years old when he received his first vision. He was living with his parents and several brothers and sisters on a farm in western New York. He was a middle child, a third son, described by his mother very frankly as "sober-minded but never very good at schoolwork."[1]

One day this child, still a teenager, comes in from the woods near his house and tells his family that he has seen a vision. In the next few years he will repeatedly claim to have been visited by angels and other heavenly messengers.

153

He will receive gold plates, which he will translate into new scripture called the Book of Mormon. He will call himself a modern prophet and restore the true Church of Christ. His claims and activities will bring tremendous pressure upon his family, including financial pressure. They will lose farms and homes. They will become subject to ridicule and violence from mobs. His older sister will feel that she was never courted by any young men in their neighborhood until she was in her twenties because of her brother. A younger sister will see her son killed by a Mormon hater twenty years after her brother died at Carthage.

Not many families could endure that kind of pressure and stay close. But Joseph's brothers and sisters stayed close to him. Even after they married and established their own families, they continued to follow Joseph as he moved his new church from western New York to Kirtland, Ohio, then to Missouri, and later to Nauvoo, Illinois.

Even more remarkable is the fact that not one of Joseph Smith's family members was ever moved to say, "Oh, come on, Joseph, who do you think you are—a prophet?" Or any words to that effect. They never said it in public, they never wrote it in their private writings. Not once, not one of them. Even William, Joseph Smith's youngest brother, who openly criticized the way Joseph handled some business and leadership affairs, never suggested that his brother was not who he said he was—even though William would leave the church that Joseph Smith founded.

There are many reasons why I am a Mormon, why I am willing to believe the rather fantastic story of how my church came to be, but one of them is because of Joseph Smith's family, because of the fact that those people who knew him so well were so steadfast in their belief and acceptance of him. I know how families work, how the differing personalities grind on each other—sometimes destroying, but more often refining each other. There is ample evidence that Joseph Smith's family functioned like that. They didn't always get along; they didn't always enjoy each other or agree with each other—except on that one essential point. And so one reason I believe Joseph Smith was a prophet is because I don't think Joseph Smith could have fooled every member of his family over a lifetime of living together if he weren't.

But that's a view of Joseph Smith that I might not have glimpsed if I had not studied his mother and his sisters who are mentioned in scripture (see JS—H 1:4, 7, 20). For me, noticing the women in scripture led me to see that God works through families to accomplish his purposes. He may speak through a particular prophet or prophetess—Moses, Joseph Smith, Abraham, Deborah, or Huldah—but those individuals cannot be separated from their families. Moses was saved by his mother and throughout his life relied upon his brother Aaron and his sister Miriam. Joseph Smith's brother Hyrum followed him even into death. Abraham was told by the Lord to go and seek counsel from his wife, Sarah. Deborah called herself a Mother in Israel, and Huldah is identified in scripture by her family and their occupation. It is not an exaggeration to say that the scriptures are a record of families starting with the first family—Adam and Eve.

155

In scripture, families come in many varieties, embracing many lifestyles. The prophetess Deborah's husband is mentioned, but the narrative focuses on her as the leader of her nation while he seems to have assumed a supportive role. The scriptures also offer examples of single-parent households and single individuals coming together to form a household. The Christian Church began in Europe in the home of a merchant woman named Lydia, who was converted and converted her household—her family—which consisted of herself and her servants. The story of Ruth and Naomi centers on two widowed women and their devotion to each other. Jesus called twelve apostles to help him preach his gospel, but it wasn't just twelve men who traveled with the Savior through the countryside carrying the message back and forth between Galilee and Jerusalem. In many cases they had their families with them. If you haven't pictured it that way, you need to reread the scriptures, carefully noticing the women. Examples are Salome, the mother of James and John, who requested the favored places at Jesus' right and left for her sons, (Matt. 20:20–23) and Jesus' own mother and brothers (Mark 3:31–32).

At the end of the Old Testament the prophet Malachi looked to our own time and promised that before the Second Coming, Elijah would return to "turn the heart of the fathers to the children, and the heart of the children to their fathers, lest I come and smite the earth with a curse" (Mal. 4:6). A curse? What curse?

Joseph Smith answered that question when he gave the Church directions about baptizing the dead. He explained that a curse would come to the earth unless a welding link was forged between the fathers and the children. He equated that link to baptism for the dead, which by extension goes on to include other temple work and the sealing of families. He went on to elaborate on the absolute necessity of family, saying, "We cannot be made perfect; neither can they without us" (D&C 128:18). In simple words, we need each other.

I called my brother long-distance and told him about the crickets in the library. He laughed. Why not? He was three thousand miles away and hadn't spent half the morning in the dean of discipline's office. But he was right. I'd let the situation become too serious. I needed to lighten up. Laughing with my brother put it all back into perspective. Family does that for us. Enmeshed in the everyday, we sometimes lose sight of the eternal. The problem is not short-sightedness. Quite the opposite. The everyday is eternity in the making, but we muddle along acting as though we think the here and now is somehow in our way, blocking us from better things.

I think that was what the Savior was trying to tell us when he sat a child in the midst of his disciples and said, "Except ye be converted, and become as little children, ye shall not enter into the kingdom of heaven" (Matt. 18:3). Two days ago I followed a group of kindergarten children through the American Museum of Natural History. They flitted here and there and everywhere, as interested in the glass cases and how the trash can lids worked as in the golden Buddhas from Japan or the t'anghas from Tibet. I could not help marveling at the children's obvious delight—their all-encompassing curiosity and love of life. I wondered if such single-minded enthusiasm is the real focus described in the scriptures as the "strait gate" and the "narrow path."

157

That was an important observation for me. I had been troubled by all those scriptures about the strait gate and narrow path. I'm sure you know the verses. Nephi in his vision of the tree of life saw a narrow road running beside the iron rod. Jesus described the way to eternal life as entering the "strait gate" and following the "narrow way." He used that image in his Sermon on the Mount, again when he visited the Nephites, and yet again as he explained exaltation to Joseph Smith in what became Doctrine and Covenants 132. In every case, he also added the warning that few would find the "narrow path" and "strait gate." That was the part that worried me.

For there was nothing in my life experience that felt like a strait gate or a narrow path. Quite the contrary. Sometimes I felt like I was traveling several paths at once. One moment I'd be a professor making out grades. Then I'd switch and function as a wife, the stake education counselor in Relief Society, a writer, a sympathetic ear for a friend, a taxi driver for my kids . . . Often I felt I was trying to be too many things all at once—a feeling that can overwhelm and confuse one's sense of direction.

From the broader perspective, I saw cycles, not narrow paths. The student who was finishing her formal education was beginning her motherhood; the mother who saw her children growing to independence was beginning a new career and going back to being a student again. Finding myself starting over repeatedly did not enhance my sense of making progress. Sometimes I wondered if I was getting anywhere at all. I even entertained the idea that I hadn't found that "strait gate." If only I could! Then surely things would straighten out and the way seem clearer.

Such simplicity is wishful thinking. In the Book of Mormon, Helaman explains the strait gate and narrow path with detail that fits the convolutions of my own experience. He says:

> . . . the gate of heaven is open unto all, even to those who will believe on the name of Jesus Christ, who is the Son of God.
>
> Yea, we see that whosoever will may lay hold upon the word of God, which is quick and powerful, which shall divide asunder all the cunning and the snares and the wiles of the devil, and lead the man [or woman] of Christ in a strait and narrow course across that everlasting gulf of misery which is prepared to engulf the wicked—
>
> And land their souls, yea, their immortal souls, at the right hand of God in the kingdom of heaven, to sit down with Abraham, and Isaac, and with Jacob, and with all our holy fathers [and our holy mothers, Eve, Sarah, Rebekah—see D&C 138:39] to go no more out. (Hel. 3:28–30)

I interpret that to mean that whatever pattern I choose for my life—whatever role I might be playing at the moment—the "strait and narrow course" Helaman describes can still be my guide, leading me from wherever I am to where I want to be. The "words of Christ" can give meaning and bring together all the diverse stands of my life into a completed whole. I find comfort in that. For when I'm not feeling overwhelmed, I enjoy the diversity of my life. When I don't think I have to prove that I've made "progress," I enjoy the excitement and challenge of starting anew.

The scriptures can be studied many ways, and ought to be studied with varied approaches in order to sample the range of what the sacred texts have to offer. I suppose there may be some who would argue that studying the basic gospel concepts of faith, repentance, etc., might be more worthwhile than focusing on the women found in scripture which is my favorite angle. I won't argue with that. I read with that kind of focus sometimes.

But at the same time, I do not underestimate the value of knowing the women. It was only through a study of my sisters in scriptures that I began to feel confident about the various directions of my own life. It was through a study of the women in the scriptures that I achieved a large enough perspective to finally understand that "strait gate" and "narrow path" and how to set my own feet upon that roadway.

You may find another way, but I'm glad mine has included getting to know Eve, Mary, Abish, Priscilla, Jehosheba, Tamar, Lydia, Rahab, Rachel, and all the others.

They've made excellent traveling companions enriching the journey. I've come to consider them family in a very real sense.

Note
1 Lucy Mack Smith, *History of Joseph Smith by his Mother* (Salt Lake City: Bookcraft, 1979), p. 17.

Index of Names

(with chapter numbers)

INDEX BY CHAPTER

165